Housing and human

Christopher Baker is a barrister at Arden Chambers in London. He specialises in housing and local government work, including human rights issues. He is the general editor of *Human Rights Act 1998: A Practitioner's Guide* (Sweet & Maxwell, 1998), co-author of *Housing Law: Pleadings in Practice* (Sweet & Maxwell, 1994), and editor of the *Encyclopedia of Local Government Law* and of the *Local Government Law Reports* (both Sweet & Maxwell). He also writes regularly for *Solicitors Journal* on housing and local government issues.

David Carter is a barrister at Arden Chambers in London. He specialises in housing and local government work, including human rights issues, having previously worked in a law centre. He is a member of the Housing and Land Sub-committee of the Civil Justice Council. He is an editor of the *Encyclopedia of Housing Law and Practice*, the *Housing Law Reports*, the *Journal of Housing Law*, the law reports in *Health and Housing Insight* (for the Chartered Institute of Environmental Health Officers) and the legal update in *Housing* (for the Chartered Institute of Housing). He is co-author of *Quiet Enjoyment (5th edn)* (Legal Action Group), *Local Authority Notices* (Sweet & Maxwell) and a contributor to *Human Rights Act 1998: A Practitioner's Guide* (Sweet & Maxwell).

Caroline Hunter is a barrister at Arden Chambers in London and senior lecturer in housing law at Sheffield Hallam University. She is the deputy general editor of the *Housing Law Reports*, *Encyclopedia of Housing Law and Practice* and the *Journal of Housing Law*. She is joint author of *Homelessness and Allocations* (Legal Action Group) and the *Manual of Housing Law* (Sweet & Maxwell).

Housing and human rights law

Christopher Baker, David Carter
and Caroline Hunter

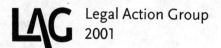 Legal Action Group
2001

This edition published in Great Britain 2001
by LAG Education and Service Trust Ltd
242 Pentonville Road
London
N1 9UN

British Library Cataloguing in Publication Data
A CIP catalogue record for this book is available from the British Library

ISBN 1 903307 05 8

Typeset by Regent Typesetting, London
Printed in Great Britain by Bell & Bain Ltd, Glasgow

Foreword

by MARTIN PARTINGTON, Law Commissioner for England and Wales

The coming into force of the Human Rights Act 1998 in October 2000 involved a step into the unknown. How would our domestic courts respond to challenges based on the provisions of the European Convention for the Protection of Human Rights and Fundamental Freedoms, the decisions of the European Commission of Human Rights and the jurisprudence of the European Court of Human Rights in Strasbourg?

The evidence to date suggests that the UK courts are, in general, adopting a cautious approach. Many of the more fanciful arguments being floated before the HRA 1998 became effective have not been taken up in practice. However, there can be no doubt that in significant respects, UK law – both procedural and substantive – has been changed.

This book is the first to explore in a clear and detailed way the potential implications of human rights law specifically on the regulation of the housing market. It adopts a measured approach, focussing on arguments that are genuinely difficult and worth pursuing. It is designed as a practical book to help those whose jobs it is to advise residential landlords and tenants – in both public and private sectors – of their legal rights and obligations. I am sure it will provide an invaluable and authoritative analysis of the impact of human rights law and practice on housing law.

I know that, as the Law Commission develops its current project on the reform of housing law, it will be relied upon to ensure that any proposals for the reform of housing law are fully compatible with the principles of the European Convention.

I am delighted to welcome this book and to wish it every success.

7 August 2001

Preface

When the Human Rights Act 1998 came fully into force on 2 October 2000, there was a great deal of speculation as to the impact it would have. Housing law was one of the key areas in which that speculation was focussed. The need for an accessible explanation of the Act and the Convention rights, and their significance to housing law, was clear.

This book has been written over the subsequent ten month period. In that time, judicial decisions in domestic courts have brought some clarity and resolved some of the speculation. A good deal more case-law has still to come. There comes a time, however, when it is necessary to be satisfied with – and to describe – what there is, rather than continue waiting for yet further developments. We feel that this moment has arrived, even though we are presently awaiting judgment from the Court of Appeal in the important cases of *R (on the application of McLellan) v Bracknell Forest DC* and *Reigate and Banstead BC v Forrest*.

The division of the book into three parts reflects the need to deal with three key aspects of the relationship between housing and human rights law. The first, written by Christopher Baker, explains the human rights which are relevant to housing. The second, written by Caroline Hunter, considers the possible impact of those rights on various practical areas of housing law. The third, written by David Carter, explains how to take and address human rights points using the mechanism of the Act.

We would like to thank and commiserate with our families, friends and colleagues for the burdens we have put on them. We received particular inspiration from Andrew Arden QC, Josephine Henderson and John McCafferty in our chambers; and warm encouragement and help from the staff at Legal Action Group.

Christopher Baker
Caroline Hunter
David Carter

Arden Chambers,
London
July 2001

Contents

Table of cases

Table of statutes

Table of statutory instruments

Table of European legislation

Abbreviations

AIA 1999	Asylum and Immigration Act 1999
CA 1989	Children Act 1989
The Convention	European Convention on Human Rights
CPR	Civil Procedure Rules
EComHR	European Commission on Human Rights
ECtHR	European Court of Human Rights
EHRR	European Human Rights Reports
HA 1985	Housing Act 1985
HA 1988	Housing Act 1988
HA 1996	Housing Act 1996
HAA 1985	Housing Associations Act 1985
HAT	Housing action trust
HRA 1998	Human Rights Act 1998
LGA 1985	Local Government Act 1985
RIPA 2000	Regulation of Investigatory Powers Act 2000
RSL	Registered social landlord
UNCESCR	United Nations Committee on Economic, Social and Cultural Rights
UNHCHR	United Nations High Commissioner for Human Rights

Convention law and housing

Introduction

Structure of Part 1

1.1   The chapters contained in this Part fall into three groups:

- Chapter 1 is an introduction identifying:
  - how international human rights law in general is concerned with housing issues;
  - the context within which the European Convention on Human Rights (the Convention)[1] has created rights applicable to housing;
  - the essential practical approach to using Convention rights in general; and
  - the key Convention rights in housing cases.
- Chapters 2 to 5 deal with the key Convention rights, considering them in detail, with reference to the case law on each.
- Chapter 6 contains the general principles which are applicable to the interpretation and use of the Convention rights.

International human rights and housing

1.2   The Convention does not exist or operate in isolation from other systems of law. It protects rights which were first established in the Universal Declaration of Human Rights 1948. Apart from reflecting the trends apparent from the domestic legal systems of the member states of the Convention, the development and application of the Convention rights also take place and are sometimes inspired[2] by the increasingly detailed network of other international human rights treaties.

Sources of housing rights

1.3   International human rights law has consistently recognised the role of housing within the framework of fundamental rights. Thus, Universal Declaration of Human Rights 1948, article 25.1 provides:

> Everyone has the right to a standard of living adequate for the health and well-being of himself and his family, including food, clothing, housing and medical care and necessary social services ...

---

1   Throughout this book 'the Convention' refers to the ECHR.
2   For example, see *Niemitz v Germany* (1992) Series A No 251–B; 16 EHRR 97, ECtHR.

1.4 Similarly, International Covenant on Economic, Social and Cultural Rights 1966, article 11 provides:

> The States Parties to the present Covenant recognize the right of everyone to an adequate standard of living for himself and his family, including adequate food, clothing and housing, and to the continuous improvement of living conditions.

1.5 There are many other provisions of international human rights treaties which are concerned with housing. These include:

- International Convention on the Elimination of All Forms of Discrimination 1965 article 5(e)(iii);
- Convention on the Elimination of All Forms of Discrimination Against Women 1979 article 14.2(h);
- Convention on the Rights of the Child 1989 article 27.3;
- Convention Relating to the Status of Refugees 1951 article 21;
- International Convention on the Protection of the Rights of All Migrant Workers and Members of their Families 1990 article 43.1;
- European Social Charter 1961 (revised 1996) article 31;
- Charter of Fundamental Rights of the European Union 2000 article 7.

Link between housing and other rights

1.6 In relation to the link between housing and human rights, the United Nations High Commissioner for Human Rights (UNHCHR) has observed:

> At first glance, it might seem unusual that a subject such as housing would constitute an issue of human rights. However, a closer look at international and national laws, as well as at the significance of a secure place to live for human dignity, physical and mental health and overall quality of life, begins to reveal some of the human rights implications of housing. Adequate housing is universally viewed as one of the most basic human needs.[3]

1.7 The UNHCHR recognises that housing both relies on and supports other human rights.[4] Various other rights (such as respect for privacy, and security of the person) are also necessary in order that one can enjoy a right to adequate housing. At the same time, having access to adequate, safe and secure housing substantially strengthens the likelihood of people being able to enjoy other rights. In his final

3 UNHCHR Fact Sheet No 21, 1997.
4 Human rights are indivisible and inter-dependent.

report the United Nations Special Rapporteur stressed the crucial importance of housing issues in human rights terms, and his deep 'regrets that housing rights have unjustifiably remained a sadly empty promise for far too many people'.[5]

Categories of housing rights

1.8   Housing rights, in a human rights context, are capable of wide definition. The UN Committee on Economic, Social and Cultural Rights (UNCESCR) has said:

> The right to housing should not be interpreted in a narrow or restrictive sense which equates it with, for example, the shelter provided by merely having a roof over one's head. Rather it should be seen as the right to somewhere to live in security, peace and dignity.[6]

Accordingly, the UNCESCR has grouped housing rights in terms of a variety of issues:

- security of tenure;
- availability of services, materials and infrastructure (ie, water, energy for cooking, heating and lighting, sanitation and washing facilities, food storage facilities, refuse disposal, drainage, and emergency services);
- affordable housing (including housing subsidies and rent controls);
- habitable housing;
- accessible housing (ie, securing full and sustainable access to housing resources, particularly for disadvantaged groups);
- location (ie, housing in a location which allows access to employment, welfare resources, schools and social facilities; and not building housing on polluted sites or near pollution sources which threaten health);
- culturally adequate housing (ie, the manner of construction, materials and underlying policies must enable the expression of cultural identity and diversity).

European law

1.9   Although European Union law recognises and gives effect to fundamental human rights, particularly those rights protected by the

5   *The Right to Adequate Housing*, para 151, 1995.
6   General Comment No 4.

Convention, this is both distinct from the Convention and of little significance in housing terms. The effect of the Convention through European law is indirect because, at present, the Union is not itself a party to the Convention and cannot become a member without a treaty amendment.[7] The manner in which European law therefore gives effect to the Convention is to use principles of fundamental human rights when applying and interpreting provisions of European law.[8] The scope of these latter provisions, however, has not extended to any substantive involvement in housing matters:[9] the law of landlord and tenant, for example, has been held to be outside the scope of European law.[10]

The Convention and housing

1.10 The main focus of the Convention has traditionally been said to be on civil and political rights (liberty of the person, freedom of speech, etc) rather than on rights of a social and economic character of which housing is a prime example. For example, the Convention has been held not to cover the right to a home,[11] or to a job.[12]

1.11 While, therefore, recognising the predominant focus and general limits of the Convention, it would however be a mistake not to acknowledge the very real application which the Convention has in a pre-eminently social and economic field such as housing. First, as a matter of generality, the ECtHR has emphasised that there is no 'watertight division' separating Convention rights from other social and economic rights.[13] Thus, many of the Convention rights have implications of a social or economic nature. Second, a number of the Convention rights have direct relevance to housing issues (see

7 Opinion 2/94 [1996] ECR I–1759, ECJ.
8 See *Charter of Fundamental Rights of the European Union 2000*; Treaty on European Union 1992 article 6(1); Opinion 2/94, above; *ERT v Pliroforissis and Kouvelas* Case C–260/89 [1991] ECR I–2925, ECJ.
9 There may be some impact, however, from other areas, such as consumer protection (see EC Treaty 1957 article 153) where general provisions may be applicable to the relationship of land-owner and occupier. See, eg, the Unfair Terms in Consumer Contracts Regulations 1999, SI No 2083, derived from European consumer legislation.
10 *R v Ministry of Agriculture, Fisheries and Food ex p Bostock* [1994] 3 CMLR 547, ECJ.
11 *Chapman v UK* (2001) 10 BHRC 48, ECtHR. See further para 2.5 onwards.
12 *X v Denmark* (1976) 3 DR 153, EComHR.
13 *Airey v Ireland* (1979) Series A No 32; 2 EHRR 305, para 26, ECtHR.

below). It is important, however, to be aware of the limits to which the
Convention rights have been applied.

Practical approach to Convention rights

1.12   In general terms, the approach to using the Convention rights
depends upon three stages of analysis:

- Is any Convention right applicable?
- Has there been an interference with, or denial or limitation of, that
  right?
- Can the interference, denial or limitation be justified, where this is
  permissible?

1.13   The first stage is a question of the legal scope of each Convention
right. The second stage is primarily a question of fact as to whether
the conduct of the state has amounted to an apparent infringement of
that right.[14] The third stage recognises that, in most cases, the
Convention rights are not absolute[15] and have to be balanced against
competing interests, including other Convention rights. The third
stage therefore involves a legal judgment about whether, on the facts,
the apparent infringement ought to be permitted. An unjustified
interference gives rise to an incompatibility with Convention rights
for the purposes of the Human Rights Act 1998.

1.14   The analysis is slightly different in cases of positive obligations.[16]
In respect of such an obligation, the issue is whether the state has
failed to take certain action, which was necessary in order to secure
the enjoyment of the relevant Convention right. Such a case involves
a legal judgment as to whether, on the facts, the Convention required
the state to take action. In considering Convention rights relevant to
housing law,[17] this involves balancing competing interests – in a way
similar to that necessary when considering whether there is
justification for interference with a Convention right.[18]

---

14   This may involve considering whether, in the particular circumstances, there
has been a waiver of the Convention right: see para 6.27 onwards.

15   A few Convention rights have, to a greater or lesser extent, an 'absolute' quality
to them: see para 6.15, below. The main Convention rights applicable to
housing, however, fit the three-stage model described above.

16   See para 6.8 and following, below.

17   In particular, article 8.

18   *Lopez Ostra v Spain* (1994) Series A No 303–C; 20 EHRR 277, para 51, ECtHR.

Key Convention rights

Article 8

1.15 The Convention provision most obviously applicable in housing cases will be article 8:

> 1. Everyone has the right to respect for his private and family life, his home and his correspondence.
> 2. There shall be no interference by a public authority with the exercise of this right except such as is in accordance with the law and is necessary in a democratic society in the interests of national security, public safety or the economic well-being of the country, for the prevention of disorder or crime, for the protection of health or morals, or for the protection of the rights and freedoms of others.

Article 1/1

1.16 Article 1 of the First Protocol is also important, often running parallel with article 8:

> Every natural or legal person is entitled to the peaceful enjoyment of his possessions. No one shall be deprived of his possessions except in the public interest and subject to the conditions provided for by law and by the general principles of international law.
> The preceding provisions shall not, however, in any way impair the right of a State to enforce such laws as it deems necessary to control the use of property in accordance with the general interest or to secure the payment of taxes or other contributions or penalties.

Article 6

1.17 At a procedural level, article 6(1) is important:

> In the determination of his civil rights and obligations or of any criminal charge against him, everyone is entitled to a fair and public hearing within a reasonable time by an independent and impartial tribunal established by law. Judgment shall be pronounced publicly but the press and public may be excluded from all or part of the trial in the interest of morals, public order or national security in a democratic society, where the interests of juveniles or the protection of the private life of the parties so require, or to the extent strictly necessary in the opinion of the court in special circumstances where publicity would prejudice the interests of justice.

Article 14

1.18   These substantive and procedural rights are supported in particular by article 14:

> The enjoyment of the rights and freedoms set forth in this Convention shall be secured without discrimination on any ground such as sex, race, colour, language, religion, political or other opinion, national or social origin, association with a national minority, property, birth or other status.

Other rights

1.19   A housing case may occasionally engage the application of other Convention rights as well,[19] and by focusing here on the rights which will ordinarily apply it should not be thought that the remainder of the Convention can be ignored. For discussion of the other Convention rights generally, the reader should refer elsewhere.[20]

---

19   For example, in a case giving rise to serious personal injury or ill-treatment, article 3 might be relied upon. It should be noted, however, that article 3 requires a high level of severity: in *Lopez Ostra v Spain* (1995) Series A No 303–C; 20 EHRR 277, ECtHR, fumes and smells were held not to have reached the necessary threshold.

20   See, for example, *European Human Rights Law*, Starmer, (LAG, 1999); *Human Rights Act 1998: A practitioner's guide*, Baker, ed, (Sweet & Maxwell, 1998).

CHAPTER 2

Article 8 – Right to respect for private and family life

continued

Introduction

1. Everyone has the right to respect for his private and family life, his home and his correspondence.
2. There shall be no interference by a public authority with the exercise of this right except such as is in accordance with the law and is necessary in a democratic society in the interests of national security, public safety or the economic well-being of the country, for the prevention of disorder or crime, for the protection of health or morals, or for the protection of the rights and freedoms of others

Scope of chapter

2.1   This chapter explains the scope of article 8, what constitutes interference with this Convention right, and whether such interference can be justified. Article 8 is likely to be the principal Convention right relied upon by occupiers. Primarily, it will be relevant to tenants and licensees, but it also applies to resident landlords and owner-occupiers.

Structure of article 8

2.2   Article 8 is unusual in its formulation. There is not a direct right to the home (and the other aspects of personal life covered by the article), but a right to *respect* for it. This can be contrasted with the first draft of the Convention, which reflected the Universal Declaration of Human Rights article 12:

No one shall be subjected to arbitrary interference with his privacy, family home or correspondence ... Everyone has the right to protection of the law against such interference ...

Respect

2.3   The effect of article 8 being formulated as it is, by reference to the notion of respect, is both to narrow and extend the scope of this right. There is a narrowing of the right in that article 8 does not, in terms, create a right to a home.[1] An extension of the right arises, however, in that the notion of respect has consistently been held to be capable of giving rise to 'positive obligations' on the part of the state.[2]

1   See para 2.5 onwards.
2   See para 2.12 onwards.

Bundle of rights

2.4   It is important to recall that article 8 protects a bundle of rights, and not merely the right to respect for the home. These rights overlap, and it is possible that a number of them may all apply in any given case.[3] In a housing context, it may be relevant to consider whether a person's private and family life[4] may be affected, even though an existing home is not in issue. Reliance on the broader aspects of article 8 is likely to be particularly important in cases of homelessness and in matters of housing allocation, where the person does not yet have a home to which respect can be accorded.[5]

No general right to a home

General position

2.5   The Strasbourg case-law has reflected the literal wording of article 8, which requires a person to have 'his' home before respect can be accorded to it. The case-law has thus consistently fallen short of recognising a right *to* a home. In *X v Federal Republic of Germany*,[6] an East German refugee in the Cold War era sought to establish that there was a breach of article 8 through the failure of the West German government to provide him with a decent home. The application was held to be inadmissible because of the wording of article 8.[7]

2.6   This general approach has received recent affirmation in *Chapman v UK*,[8] where the ECtHR held that there had been no violation of article 8 in relation to the use of planning enforcement procedures against the applicant, who had stationed gypsy caravans on her land in breach of planning law. The ECtHR observed:[9]

3   For example, see *Chapman v UK* (2001) 10 BHRC 48, paras 71–74, ECtHR; reported with *Coster v UK* App No 24876/94; *Beard v UK*, App No 24882/94; *Lee v UK* App No 25289/94; and *Smith v UK* App No 15154/94.

4   See para 2.29 onwards.

5   See also para 2.12 onwards.

6   (1956) 1 YB 202, EComHR.

7   See also *Y v Federal Republic Germany* App No 1340/62, EcomHR; *X v Federal Republic of Germany* (1967) 23 CD 51, EComHR. In *Smith v UK* App No 14455/88, which arose from a domestic law challenge under the Caravan Sites Act 1968, the Commission observed that article 8 did not contain 'an express right to living accommodation'.

8   See note 3 above.

9   At para 99 of the judgment.

It is important to recall that article 8 does not in terms give a right to be provided with a home. Nor does any of the jurisprudence of the court acknowledge such a right. While it is clearly desirable that every human being has a place where he or she can live in dignity and which he or she can call home, there are unfortunately in the contracting states many persons who have no home. Whether the state provides funds to enable everyone to have a home is a matter for political not judicial decision.

2.7 This is consistent with the manner in which the UN authorities approach the matter. The UN Special Rapporteur[10] has taken the view that housing rights, at the most basic level, do not imply that the state is required to build housing for the entire population, or that the state must necessarily fulfil all aspects of the right to housing imme-diately upon assuming duties to do so.

Further examples

2.8 This limitation on the scope of article 8 has also found reflection in other cases. In *Strunjak v Croatia*,[11] it was held that the failure to provide private sector tenants with the right to buy, when public sec-tor tenants did enjoy this right, did not fall within article 8. The right only protects a person's right to respect for an existing home, and does not include a right to buy a home.[12] Similarly, in *Velosa Barretto v Portugal*,[13] a landlord failed in the attempt to rely upon article 8 in challenging the refusal of the domestic courts to terminate the tenant's lease. The landlord and his family lived in accommodation rented by his wife's parents, and other members of his wife's family lived there also. Subsequently, he inherited a house which was leased to a tenant. The landlord applied unsuccessfully to the domestic courts to terminate the lease so that his family could live in the house. Relying on the right to respect for private and family life, the landlord claimed that it was implicit in article 8 that each family had the right to a home for themselves alone. The court held, however, that:

> ... effective respect for private and family life cannot require the existence in national law of legal protection enabling each family to

---

10 See para 1.7.

11 App No 46934/99, ECtHR.

12 This can be compared with the position under article 1/1, which protects possessions but not the right to obtain possessions: see para 3.5, below.

13 (1996) Series A No 334; [1996] EHRLR 212, ECtHR.

have a home for themselves alone. It does not go so far as to place the State under an obligation to give a landlord the right to recover possession of a rented house on request and in any circumstances.[14]

Exceptions: positive obligations

2.9   There does remain, however, some scope in particular cases for arguing that article 8 creates a positive obligation on the state to provide housing assistance where this is necessary in order to secure respect for a person's private and family life (see below). The Strasbourg case-law is not yet well-developed in this regard, and there is scope for further development and clarification. This promises to be a crucial area of future challenge, determining the effective scope of article 8.

Factual issues

2.10   Factual issues can arise as to whether a person is seeking to protect an existing home, or whether the complaint relates merely to an attempt to establish a home. In *Buckley v UK*,[15] the government sought to argue that the applicant was merely seeking the right to establish a home in relation to gypsy caravans which had been stationed on her land in contravention of planning control. The Commission and the ECtHR held that the caravans on the land did constitute a home, even though the legal right to station them on the land had not been established.

Welfare benefits

2.11   In *UA and MK v Sweden*,[16] the Commission considered a complaint arising from a refusal of welfare benefit in respect of a young family. It was held that the Convention did not guarantee the right to public assistance, either in the form of financial support or in the form of supplying home care places. It was also held that the right to respect for family life did not extend to impose on states a general obligation to provide for financial assistance to individuals in order to enable one of two parents to stay at home to take care of children. As with the

14   At para 24. See also *Reuter v Germany*, App No 32009/96, EComHR.

15   RJD 1996–IV 1271; 23 EHRR 101, paras 52–54 of judgment, and paras 61–63 of Commission report.

16   (1986) 46 DR 251, EComHR.

absence of any general right to a home, however, some scope may arise in cases of particular need to rely upon the existence of a positive obligation.[17]

Positive obligations[18]

2.12 It is clear from Strasbourg case-law that article 8 recognises the existence of some positive obligations on the state. Whereas the Convention is mainly concerned with (negatively) restraining interference by the state in the enjoyment of rights, in certain cases the state may (positively) be called upon to take action in order to secure and protect a person's enjoyment of those rights. In the context of article 8, the scope for positive obligations arises from the notion of 'respect'.

Uncertain scope of 'respect'

2.13 What is to be comprised within the notion of respect very much depends on the particular context, and this is an uncertain and developing area of jurisprudence. The concept of respect is not precisely defined: it has consistently been said not to be 'clear-cut'.[19] In order to determine whether positive obligations exist, it is necessary to have regard to the fair balance which must be struck between the general interest and the interests of the individual; and in striking this balance the state has a margin of appreciation.[20] The degree of consensus between Convention states, practical considerations (including expert and scientific evidence), and the seriousness of the effect on the individual are all relevant considerations.[21]

Established examples

2.14 In a housing context, the Strasbourg authorities have been relatively slow to acknowledge the existence of positive obligations, but several more recent cases demonstrate a developing momentum. In *Powell*

---

17 See para 2.12 onwards.
18 See generally para 6.8 onwards.
19 See, for example, *Abdulaziz, Cabales and Balkandali v UK* (1985) Series A No 94; 7 EHRR 471, para 67, ECtHR.
20 *Botta v Italy* (1998) 26 EHRR 241, para 33, ECtHR.
21 For example, *Sheffield and Horsham v UK* (1998) 27 EHRR 163, ECtHR.

and Rayner v UK,[22] the ECtHR was willing to accept that there might be a positive obligation on the government in relation to regulating interference by aircraft noise (in that case from Heathrow airport). In *Whiteside v UK*,[23] a case involving harassment[24] in and around the home by a former cohabitee, the Commission held that there was a positive obligation on the government 'to secure the applicant's rights by providing adequate protection against this type of deliberate persecution'. The positive obligation of the state to take action in relation to serious environmental pollution has now clearly been recognised in cases such as *Lopez Ostra v Spain*,[25] concerning fumes and smells from a waste treatment plant affecting a residential area, and which is a relatively rare example of the ECtHR finding a violation of a positive obligation under article 8. Similarly, in *Guerra v Italy*,[26] the ECtHR found that the direct effect of toxic emissions from a factory gave rise to a positive duty to communicate information to enable inhabitants to assess the risks.

Requirement for direct link

2.15   Reviewing a number of the authorities in *Botta v Italy*,[27] the ECtHR observed that positive obligations arose under article 8 where there was 'a direct and immediate link between the measures sought by an applicant and the latter's private and/or family life'.[28] In that case, however, the ECtHR held that the nature of the right sought to be established by the applicant was not capable of falling within this fairly stringent test. The applicant was physically disabled, and was seeking to establish a right to facilities enabling access to a beach during holidays; but this was both geographically distant from his home and involved 'interpersonal relations of ... broad and indeterminate scope', so that there was held to be no 'direct link' of the sort required.

---

22 (1990) Series A No 172; 12 EHRR 355, ECtHR.
23 (1994) 76A DR 80, EComHR.
24 The county court judge had followed *Patel v Patel* [1988] 2 FLR 179, CA, in refusing an application for interlocutory relief, on the grounds that there was no tort of harassment. The position in domestic law subsequently developed and changed, by reason of *Khorasandjian v Bush* [1993] QB 727, CA, and the Protection from Harassment Act 1997.
25 (1995) Series A No 303–C; 20 EHRR 277, ECtHR.
26 (1998) 26 EHRR 357, ECtHR.
27 (1998) 26 EHRR 241, ECtHR.
28 See para 34.

Homelessness

2.16 Perhaps the most important recognition to date of a positive obligation to provide housing assistance has come in *Marzari v Italy*.[29] In that case, the ECtHR considered the admissibility of a claim from an applicant who suffered from severe disability. The applicant had been evicted for his refusal to pay rent, having contended that his public sector apartment did not meet his needs. He lived in a camper van, and his health deteriorated considerably. He then refused an offer of accommodation, which the medical experts said would be suitable, and in relation to which the municipal authority agreed to pay the rent. The ECtHR held that:

> ... although article 8 does not guarantee the right to have one's housing problem solved by the authorities, a refusal of the authorities to provide assistance in this respect to an individual suffering from a severe disease might in some circumstances raise an issue under article 8 of the Convention because of the impact of such refusal on the private life of the individual.[30]

Limited extent of obligation

2.17 While the existence of the positive obligation was recognised by the ECtHR in *Marzari*, the limitation of that obligation was also identified. The eviction of the applicant was held to have been justified in the circumstances, and the ECtHR held that it would not interfere with decisions on the suitability of accommodation. In particular, it held that 'no positive obligation for the local authorities can be inferred from article 8 to provide the applicant with a specific apartment'.

2.18 Similarly, in *Burton v UK*,[31] the Commission did not consider that article 8 could 'be interpreted in such a way as to extend a positive obligation to provide alternative accommodation of an applicant's choosing'. The applicant, who suffered from cancer, complained that, in failing to provide her with a place where she could live out her days in a caravan according to her Romany background, the local authority had failed in their obligation under article 8. The Commission rejected her application.

---

29 (1999) 28 EHRR CD175, ECtHR.
30 This statement of principle was reiterated in the joint dissenting opinion of seven judges in *Chapman v UK* (2001) 10 BHRC 48, ECtHR, when challenging the relevance or validity of the ruling by the majority cited at para 2.6 above.
31 (1996) 22 EHRR CD 135.

Horizontal effect

2.19   One consequence of a positive obligation, once established, is that the Convention right may cease to be purely a question of the relations between the state and the individual. The obligation may also involve the adoption of measures for the regulation of relations between individuals, or so-called horizontal effect.[32] An example is the obligation to provide protection against harassment.[33]

What is a home?

2.20   The term 'home' in article 8 has an autonomous meaning[34] under the Convention, which does not depend upon the classification in domestic law. Nonetheless, the Convention concept follows a pattern which is familiar to domestic law.

General definition

2.21   In general terms, a home is where a person lives on a settled basis, which requires a degree of stability and continuity.[35] The concept depends upon the factual circumstances in each case, namely the existence of sufficient and continuous links between the person and the property.[36]

Requirement of occupation

2.22   It is necessary that the person has lived in the property.[37] It is not sufficient for the purposes of article 8 for a person to show ownership of certain property,[38] even with an intention to create a home there. Thus, in *Loizidou v Turkey*,[39] the applicant intended to build a block of flats on her land in northern Cyprus, but was unable to do so because of the military occupation by Turkey. Even though one of the flats was intended to be for the use of the applicant's own family, the ECtHR

---

32   *X and Y v Netherlands* (1985) Series A No 91; 8 EHRR 235, ECtHR.
33   See *Whiteside v UK*, at para 2.14 above.
34   For this term generally, see para 6.5 below.
35   See *Wiggins v UK* (1978) 13 DR 40, EComHR.
36   See *Buckley v UK* (1995) 19 EHRR CD20, EComHR.
37   See *Potocka v Poland* App No 33776/96, ECtHR.
38   See *Gillow v UK* (1984) 7 EHRR 292, para 116, EComHR.
39   (1995) Series A No 310; 20 EHRR 99, ECtHR.

held that 'it would strain the meaning of the notion of "home" in article 8 to extend it to comprise property on which it is proposed to build a house for residential purposes'. Similarly, where the applicants were in the process of having a house built on an island, and there was only a construction site with building workers there, there was no home.[40] The Commission was also not satisfied that the applicant had established that a house was his home, when as owner he let out rooms in the house, retaining the ground floor for his own use and intending to occupy one of the flats in the house after the house had been converted.[41]

Absence of occupier

2.23 Once a person has established a home, however, the status of the property can survive even lengthy absences. In *Gillow v UK*,[42] the applicants had lived in a house on Guernsey, and had then moved around the world. They had a house in England, in addition to the one in Guernsey. They complained about legal restraints in Guernsey which prevented them from lawfully resuming occupation of their house there after an absence of 18 years. The Commission rejected the argument that the Gillows did not have a home in Guernsey. The ECtHR endorsed the Commission's approach, referring to the fact that the Gillows had retained ownership, had left furniture in the premises, and had always intended to return, and that they had thus retained 'sufficient continuing links' with the property.

Offices

2.24 The breadth of the term 'home' is such that it can extend to a professional person's office. In Germany, it has been interpreted in this way. This interpretation is consistent both with the French text of the Convention (where the term 'domicile' is used and which has a broader connotation than 'home') and with the essential object and purpose of article 8 which is to protect the individual against arbitrary interference by the state. This interpretation also recognises the fact that residential and professional user may be difficult in practice to distinguish.[43]

40 *Barclay v UK* App No 35712/97, ECtHR.
41 *Maggiulli v UK* App No 12736/87, ECtHR.
42 (1986) Series A no 109; 11 EHRR 335, ECtHR.
43 *Niemitz v Germany* (1992) Series A No 251–B; 16 EHRR 97, paras 30–31, ECtHR. In contrast, in *Fontanesi v Austria*, App No 30192/96, the court

Movable homes

2.25   Movable accommodation may constitute a home. A significant number of cases have established that occupation of a caravan, if sufficiently established, falls within the scope of article 8.[44] On the other
hand, in *Khanthak v Federal Republic of Germany*,[45] the Commission
left open whether a camper van could constitute a home.

Status of occupier

2.26   It is not entirely clear what legal interest, if any, a person must have in
the property. In *S v UK*,[46] the same-sex partner of a deceased secure
tenant, who had no personal interest in the tenancy and no right to
succeed to it, could not establish that the premises were her home
despite long-term occupation. This was a narrow view to have taken,
and it may be that it will not generally be followed. In *Khatun v UK*,[47]
for example, the Commission stressed that the concept of a home was
an autonomous one under the Convention, and held that all the
occupiers in that case could rely on article 8, whether or not they were
themselves owners or tenants of the properties in question. Thus the
partners, children, relatives and lodgers of the proprietors were
covered by article 8.

Illegal occupation

2.27   A caravan, even though it was sited illegally in contravention of
planning laws, was still a home.[48] The illegality, however, affected the
extent of the obligation on the state, and was a major factor in the

> expressed doubt whether a lawyer's right to carry on a profession could in itself
> fall within article 8. But see also *Verein Netzwerk v Austria*, App No 32549/96,
> where the court was prepared to recognise the possibility that the premises of a
> housing association, which were its offices and also home to a number of
> individuals, might be 'home'. This would seem to recognise that a non-natural
> person can take advantage of this part of article 8.

44   *Chapman v UK* (2001) 10 BHRC 48, ECtHR. See also *Buckley v UK* RJD 1996–IV
1271; 23 EHRR 101, ECtHR. Similar cases include *Lay v UK* App No 13341/87,
EComHR, and *Mabey v UK* (1996) 22 EHRR CD 123, EComHR.

45   (1988) 58 DR 94, EComHR.

46   (1986) 47 DR 274, EComHR.

47   (1998) 26 EHRR CD212, EComHR. The complaint in this case followed the
ruling of the House of Lords in *Hunter v Canary Wharf Ltd* [1997] AC 655,
which, among other things, restricted the categories of person who have the
standing to sue for nuisance.

48   See note 44 above.

finding of justification for the interference involved in the enforcement of planning controls.

Terms and conditions

2.28 The Strasbourg authorities have held that certain rights and obligations derived from a lease did not themselves fall within the scope of article 8. Thus a tenant could not use the right to respect for the home in order to challenge a 'negotiation clause', which fixed the rent and other conditions on the basis of an umbrella agreement in force between, among others, a landlords' union and a tenants' union.[49] Similarly, in *Artingstoll v UK*,[50] the Commission rejected a complaint from a council tenant in relation to a ban on keeping pets. Previous case-law had held that the keeping of pets did not fall within the scope of private life,[51] and whether or not this remained true in the light of medical evidence, the Commission held that the state could not be held responsible when the applicant had known there was a ban on keeping pets from the outset.

Private and family life

2.29 Private and family life are concepts with autonomous meanings[52] under the Convention, and which thus display independence from classification in domestic law. The concept of private life is much broader than that of privacy, although its ambit is imprecise. In *Niemitz v Germany*,[53] it was said:

> The court does not consider it possible or necessary to attempt an exhaustive definition of the notion of 'private life'. However, it would be too restrictive to limit the notion to an 'inner circle' in which the individual may live his own personal life as he chooses and to exclude therefrom entirely the outside world not encompassed within that circle. Respect for private life must also comprise to a certain degree the right to establish and develop relationships with other human beings.

49 *Langborger v Sweden* (1989) Series A No 155; 12 EHRR 416, paras 38–39, ECtHR. See also *Cunningham v Sweden*, App No 11914/86, EComHR, and *J and EH v Sweden*, app no 13347/87, EComHR, where the tenants withdrew similar challenges, following *Langborger*.
50 App No 25517/94, EComHR.
51 *X v Iceland* 5 DR 86, App No 6825/74.
52 See generally para 6.5, below.
53 (1992) Series A No 251–B, 16 EHRR 97, para 29, ECtHR.

The court held in that case the search of a lawyer's office gave rise to protection under article 8 in respect of private life, as well as in respect of the home.[54]

Disability

2.30   More recently, the court has considered the scope of private life in relation to the rights of disabled people.[55] In *Botta v Italy*,[56] the applicant was physically disabled, and complained about the lack of lavatories and ramps on a seaside holiday. Private life was held to include a person's 'physical and psychological integrity'. The ECtHR seems to have accepted that the 'interpersonal relations' linked to the applicant taking a holiday did fall within the concept of private life, but held that the scope of the positive obligation[57] contended for by the applicant was too broad and indeterminate to come within the notion of 'respect'.[58]

Pollution

2.31   Serious environmental pollution, which has direct effect on individuals, affects private and family life.[59] The well-being of individuals, and the enjoyment of their homes, may be adversely affected, and thus within the scope of private and family life, even though their health is not seriously endangered.[60]

Gypsies

2.32   In *Chapman v UK*,[61] the ECtHR held that the applicant's occupation of her caravan was an integral part of her ethnic identity as a gypsy, reflecting the long tradition of a minority following a travelling lifestyle. The enforcement of planning controls affected the applicant's ability to maintain her identity as a gypsy, and to lead her private and family life in accordance with that tradition.[62]

---

54   See also *Kopp v Switzerland* (1999) 27 EHRR 91, ECtHR.
55   See also *Marzari v Italy* (1999) 28 EHRR CD 175, ECtHR.
56   (1998) 26 EHRR 241, ECtHR.
57   See above, para 2.12.
58   See above, para 2.3.
59   *Guerra v Italy* (1998) 26 EHRR 357, ECtHR.
60   *Lopez Ostra v Spain* (1994) Series A No 303–C; 20 EHRR 277, ECtHR.
61   (2001) 10 BHRC 48, paras 72–73, ECtHR.
62   See also *Buckley v UK* RJD 1996–IV 1271; 23 EHRR 101, para 64, ECtHR.

Further examples

2.33   Private life has also been held to include questions of personal identity,[63] personal information,[64] and personal telephone calls even on business premises.[65] The storing of personal information by a public authority amounts to an interference within article 8.[66]

2.34   Family life includes relationships based on marriage, but also extends much more broadly than this to other family ties between adults and children, and stable adult relationships.[67] It is not essential that the relationship should include an element of cohabitation.[68] At present, Convention law does not recognise that same-sex relationships fall within the scope of family life,[69] though they can come within the concept of private life.

Interference[70]

2.35   It is a question of fact, relative to the scope of the obligation imposed by article 8 in each case, whether any particular act or measure amounts to an interference.

Deprivation

2.36   Deprivation of the home is clearly an interference. Extreme cases have concerned military action, such as *Cyprus v Turkey*,[71] and *Mentes v Turkey*.[72] At the other end of the scale, lawful eviction by a landlord

---

63   *B v France* (1992) Series A No 232; 16 EHRR 1, ECtHR, concerning sexual identity. See also *Burghartz v Switzerland* (1994) Series A No 280–B; 18 EHRR 101, ECtHR, concerning names.

64   *Leander v Sweden* (1987) Series A No 116; 9 EHRR 433, ECtHR. See also *Gaskin v UK* (1989) Series A No 160, 12 EHRR 36, ECtHR, concerning the right to obtain information about oneself.

65   *Halford v UK* RJD 1997–III 1004; 24 EHRR 523, ECtHR.

66   *Amann v Switzerland* (2000) 30 EHRR 843, ECtHR.

67   *Marckx v Belgium* (1979) Series A No 31; 2 EHRR 330, ECtHR; *Johnston v Ireland* (1986) Series A No 112; 9 EHRR 203, ECtHR; *Keegan v Ireland* (1994) Series A No 290; 18 EHRR 342, ECtHR.

68   *Kroon v Netherlands* (1994) Series A No 297–C; 19 EHRR 263, ECtHR.

69   See *Grant v South West Trains Ltd* Case C–249/96 [1998] ECR I–621, para 33, ECJ, and the cases there cited. English law has, however, moved forward on its own: see *Fitzpatrick v Sterling Housing Association Ltd* [2001] 1 AC 27, HL.

70   See also under article 1/1, chapter 3, below.

71   (1976) 4 EHRR 482, ECtHR.

72   (1998) 26 EHRR 595, ECtHR.

has also been held to be an interference.[73] Dispossession of the landlord by use of powers of compulsory purchase may also bring article 8 into operation, if the premises are the landlord's own home.[74] In one case, the Commission appeared to have some doubt, without finding it necessary to decide the point, whether an eviction was an interference when the local authority terminated a contractual right to occupy a caravan site in accordance with the terms of the contract.[75] But in *Ure v UK*,[76] the Commission apparently accepted that the termination of a tenancy by service of a co-tenant's notice to quit was an interference. Also, in *Lambeth LBC v Howard*,[77] Sedley LJ held that any attempt or legal threat to evict a person from their home engages the application of article 8.

Control of use

2.37   Legal measures preventing a person from using premises as a home may also clearly constitute an interference. Thus the application of planning controls to require cessation of unlawful residential use has regularly been held to constitute an interference with the right to respect for the home.[78] At a less serious level, the ECtHR did not find it necessary to decide whether the use of planning controls to require the removal or lowering of a garden fence was an interference, since it was justified in any event.[79]

Existence of laws

2.38   In general, under the Convention, it is necessary for any law to be actually applied in practice in order for there to be an interference.[80]

---

73   *Marzari v Italy* (1999) 28 EHRR CD 175, ECtHR.

74   See, for example, *Maggiulli v UK*, App No 12736/87, EComHR. In *Howard v UK* (1985) 9 EHRR 116, EComHR, the government accepted the interference arising from the use of such powers.

75   *P v UK*, App No 14751/89, where the complaint followed from the House of Lords' decision in *Powell v Greenwich LBC* [1989] AC 995. See also *Wiggins v UK* (1978) 13 DR 40, EComHR, where the Commission seemed to accept that the application of a pre-existing condition to the enjoyment of a property might not be an interference if it was foreseeable.

76   App No 28027/95, following the decision of the Court of Appeal in *Crawley BC v Ure* [1996] QB 13.

77   [2001] EWCA Civ 468, (2001) 33 HLR 58, paras 30 and 32. See also para 8.27.

78   See, for example, *Chapman v UK* (2001) 10 BHRC 48, ECtHR.

79   *Hamer v Netherlands*, App No 48857/99, ECtHR.

80   The position under the Human Rights Act 1998, however, would seem to be

Thus, in *Strunjak v Croatia*,[81] the applicants complained that new legislation had terminated their protected tenancies. The ECtHR held that there was no indication of any violation of article 8, because the tenants retained security of tenure and it would be necessary for the landlord to bring proceedings for possession. None of the applicants was subject to any such proceedings, or in any immediate danger of an eviction order, and the court would not speculate as to the outcome if proceedings were commenced. Exceptionally, the existence of legislation may be held to be sufficient in itself, but only where its existence can be said to be having some concrete and present effect on the applicant.[82]

Physical entry

2.39 Entry into the home can constitute an interference. In *McLeod v UK*,[83] police officers entered the applicant's home, in her absence, when accompanying her husband who was seeking to enforce a court order for the return of property. There was held to have been a violation of article 8. In another case, the search by officials of a room occupied by the applicant was an interference, though on the facts it was held to have been justified.[84] On the other hand, it is doubtful that entry will be an interference where it has been permitted voluntarily.[85] Unauthorised entry onto property owned by another, without more, does not necessarily entail any interference with respect for private life.[86]

Nuisance

2.40 Activities which, in domestic law, would be recognised as a nuisance are capable of giving rise to an interference because they interfere

somewhat less restrictive in two respects. First, s7(1) permits a victim to complain where a public authority merely 'proposes' to act contrary to s6. Second, legislation can itself be the subject of scrutiny and challenge under ss3 and 4; though doubtless in this instance the courts will wish to be satisfied that the claimant has standing to bring the challenge.

81 App No 46934/99, ECtHR.
82 See, for example, *Dudgeon v UK* (1981) Series A No 45; 4 EHRR 149, ECtHR. *Norris v Ireland* (1988) Series A No 142; 13 EHRR 186, ECtHR.
83 (1999) 27 EHRR 493, ECtHR.
84 *Camenzind v Switzerland* (1997) 28 EHRR 458, ECtHR.
85 *Verein Netzwerk v Austria*, App No 32549/96, ECtHR.
86 *Barclay v UK*, App No 35712/97, ECtHR.

with the enjoyment of the home. Thus aircraft noise,[87] fumes and smells from a waste treatment plant,[88] and toxic emissions from a chemical plant,[89] have all been held to fall within article 8. In *Khatun v UK*,[90] the Commission held that there had been an interference with the applicants' rights under article 8 in relation to the dust caused by the construction of the Limehouse Link tunnel in London. This was so, even though there was no allegation of ill-health, because the applicants could not open windows or dry laundry outside for a period of three years.

2.41   As with the tort of nuisance, it is a question of fact and degree whether the matters complained about are sufficient to establish an interference. In *Vearncombe v UK and Federal Republic of Germany*,[91] residents near to a British military firing range in West Berlin complained about the noise. The Commission observed that there was nothing to show that the range was used in such a manner as to cause 'continuous important noise nuisance'. Accordingly, the Commission held that it could not find that the applicants were, or could ... intolerable and exceptional noise nuisance ... cy as to amount to a possible interference. ... l of nuisance from a waste treatment plant ... less than that in *Lopez Ostra v Spain*,[93] and ... l measures had reduced the effects to the ... nience' with the effect that the applicants ... victims of any violation.

Justification of interference: generally

2.42   If there has been an interference under article 8(1), there will be a violation of the right unless the interference can be justified by the state. It is for the state to establish that any interference with the right under article 8(1) is justified. Article 8(2) is to be narrowly interpreted, because it provides for an exception to a right guaranteed by the

87 *Arrondelle v UK* (1982) 26 DR 5, EComHR (Gatwick Airport) – which the government settled by making an *ex gratia* payment. See also *Powell and Rayner v UK* (1989) Series A No 172; 12 EHRR 355, ECtHR.

88 *Lopez Ostra v Spain* (1994) Series A No 303–C; 20 EHRR 277, ECtHR.

89 *Guerra v Italy* (1998) 26 EHRR 357, ECtHR.

90 (1998) 26 EHRR CD 212, EComHR. See *Marcic v Thames Water Utilities Ltd* [2001] 3 All ER 698, QBD.

91 App No 12816/87, EComHR.

92 App No 32549/96, ECtHR.

93 See note 88 above.

Convention.[94] For the purposes of the Human Rights Act 1998, an unjustified interference will give rise to an incompatibility with the Convention right.[95]

2.43   To justify the interference, it is necessary to satisfy the requirements of article 8(2), which sets out the extent to which the state may place limitations upon the enjoyment of the Convention right. The interference must accordingly:

1) be in accordance with the law;
2) pursue a legitimate aim; and
3) be necessary in a democratic society.

Each of these is explained below. The essence of these requirements is to prevent and control arbitrary discretion and abuse of power. Because article 8(2) expressly sets out the limitations which can be placed upon the right under article 8(1), it has been held[96] that it is not possible to introduce any further limitations by implication.[97] Article 8(2) is thus exhaustive.

In accordance with the law

2.44   It is a necessary component of any justification that the particular interference must have some formal basis in law and be compliant with it.[98] Law is to be distinguished not only from illegal action, but also from mere administrative (and particularly arbitrary) discretion which is not susceptible to legal control. The recognised sources of law for this purpose include not only primary legislation, but also subordinate legislation,[99] case-law,[100] and international law.[101]

Meaning of 'law'

2.45   'Law' carries its own special meaning under the Convention, and it is not sufficient that the interference happens to be lawful in domestic law. Two additional criteria have to be satisfied. First, the legal rule or

---

94 *Klass v Federal Republic of Germany* (1978) Series A No 28; 2 EHRR 214, para 42, ECtHR.
95 Under either HRA 1998 s3 and/or s6.
96 *Golder v UK* (1975) Series A No 18; 1 EHRR 524, para 44, ECtHR.
97 For implied limitations, see para 6.18, below.
98 *Sunday Times v UK* (1979) Series A No 30; 2 EHRR 245, para 47, ECtHR.
99 *Golder v UK*, above, at para 45 of the judgment.
100 *Sunday Times v UK*, above, at para 49 of the judgment.
101 *Groppera Radio AG v Switzerland* (1990) Series A No 173; 12 EHRR 321, para 68, ECtHR.

principle must be adequately accessible to the citizen, who must thus be able to obtain an adequate indication of the legal rules applicable to a given case.[102] Unpublished or secret rules do not satisfy this requirement.[103] Second, the legal rule or principle must be formulated with sufficient precision to enable the citizen to regulate her/his conduct. S/he must be able, if necessary with appropriate advice, to foresee to a reasonable degree the consequences which a given action may entail.[104] Law which is unclear or incomplete may not satisfy this requirement.[105]

Legitimate aim

2.46   It is a required component of any justification that the particular interference must pursue one of the legitimate aims which is expressly recognised by article 8(2). In housing cases, the relevant aims among those recognised are: public safety, the economic well-being of the country, the prevention of disorder or crime, the protection of health or morals, or the protection of the rights and freedoms of others.[106] It is for the state to identify and establish the objectives.

Necessary in a democratic society

2.47   It is also a required component of any justification that the particular interference must be necessary in a democratic society. This phrase involves a number of elements which need to be identified and understood properly, because this aspect of article 8(2) is in practice the most significant.

Components

2.48   The word 'necessary' is not to be interpreted as narrowly as something indispensable; but at the other extreme it means more than merely reasonable or desirable.[107] What is required is that the inter-

---

102 *Sunday Times v UK*, above, at para 49 of the judgment.
103 See, for example, *Silver v UK* (1983) Series A No 61; 5 EHRR 347, ECtHR.
104 See note 102 above.
105 Ibid. See also *Halford v UK* (1997) 24 EHRR 523, ECtHR. *Kruslin v France* (1990) Series A No 176–A, 12 EHRR 547, ECtHR.
106 For examples, see para 2.53 onwards.
107 *Handyside v UK* (1976) Series A No 24; 1 EHRR 737, para 48, ECtHR. *Silver v UK* (1983) Series A No 61; 5 EHRR 347, para 97, ECtHR.

ference must correspond to a 'pressing social need', and it must also be proportionate to the legitimate aim which is being pursued.[108] This involves considering whether the reasons given by the state for the interference are relevant and sufficient.[109]

Margin of appreciation

2.49 Under the Convention, when it comes to the imposition of restrictions or limitations upon Convention rights, the state enjoys a certain but not unlimited area of discretion, which is referred to as the margin of appreciation.[110] Although the concept of a margin of appreciation does not have direct application in relation to the enforcement of Convention rights within domestic law, the English courts nonetheless are developing and apply an analogous concept which recognises that certain decisions are best left – up to a point – to the legislative and administrative authorities and should not be taken by the courts. The margin of appreciation thus affects the intensity with which the courts will review or supervise the measures taken by the state: the wider the margin, the less intense the review.

Varying extent of margin

2.50 The margin of appreciation varies according to the context. A number of factors are relevant: the nature of the Convention right, its importance for the individual, the nature of the activities which are restricted, the nature of the aim pursued by the restrictions, and the extent of any consensus among member states on the point at issue.[111] Economic and social factors, which have particular importance in relation to housing policy, have been accorded a wider margin of appreciation.[112]

Examples of disproportionality

2.51 In the large majority of cases concerning the home, the state has succeeded where necessary in justifying the interference under article 8.

---

108 *Handyside v UK*, above, paras 48–49 and 97 respectively.

109 See, for example, *Chapman v UK* (2001) 10 BHRC 48, para 90, ECtHR.

110 See generally para 6.20 onwards.

111 See *Chapman* at note 109 above; *Rasmussen v Denmark* (1984) Series A No 87; 7 EHRR 371, ECtHR.

112 See *Mellacher v Austria* (1989) Series A No 169; 12 EHRR 391, ECtHR. See also *R v Secretary of State for the Environment, Transport and the Regions, ex p Spath Holme Ltd* [2001] 2 WLR 15, HL.

Two exceptions to this, involving the United Kingdom, stand out. In
Gillow v UK,[113] there was held to have been an unjustified interference
under article 8 in relation to the exercise by a Guernsey housing
authority of a discretion in considering whether to grant a licence to
permit the owners of a house to occupy it. Insufficient weight was
held to have been given to the applicants' personal circumstances,
and the decisions of the authority to refuse temporary and permanent
licences were held to have been disproportionate.[114]

2.52   In *McLeod v UK*,[115] there was held to have been an unjustified
interference under article 8 when police officers entered the applicant's home and assisted the applicant's former husband in his
removal of property purportedly in compliance with a court order.
The order in fact required the applicant to deliver the property, and
did not authorise the former husband to collect it; moreover, there
were still three more days left for the applicant to comply with it. The
purpose of the police attending was to prevent a breach of the peace
(following a long and acrimonious history in divorce proceedings),
which was held to have been in accordance with the law, and in pur-
suit of a legitimate aim; but the ECtHR held that the means employed
by the police were disproportionate. The police had not checked the
terms of the court order, and they had taken for granted that the former husband was correct in saying that he had reached an agreement
with the applicant for removal of the property. In addition, the court
held that the police should not have entered the home, upon being
told by the applicant's mother that the applicant was not present,
because it should have been clear that there was little or no risk of
disorder or crime occurring.

Mandatory possession orders

2.53   The legislation in the Housing Act 1996 governing the recovery of
possession from introductory tenants (see para 4.28 for an explanation of introductory tenants) has been held to correspond to a pressing social need, having regard to the interests of other tenants and
neighbours in relation to problems of rent arrears and anti-social

---

113 (1986) Series A No 109; 11 EHRR 335, ECtHR.

114 Contrast *Walker-Bow v UK*, App No 17176/80, EComHR, where a similar
     challenge under article 1/1 in respect of controls in Jersey failed.

115 (1999) 27 EHRR 493, ECtHR. The Strasbourg application followed an
     unsuccessful action by the applicant against the police: *McLeod v Commissioner
     of Police of the Metropolis* [1994] 4 All ER 553, CA.

behaviour. The limited nature of the interference, and the difficulties involved in other methods of legal enforcement, meant that the interference was considered to be proportionate.[116] Similarly, the mandatory provisions under Housing Act 1988 s21(4) for the recovery of possession of premises let on an assured shorthold tenancy have been held to be legitimate and proportionate, and thus not in conflict with the tenant's right under article 8.[117] In that case, the existence of a procedure for the recovery of possession at the end of a tenancy was considered to be necessary in a democratic society, and the restricted power of the court in this instance was considered to be a matter of policy in which the courts should defer to Parliament.

Other eviction cases

2.54 In relation to possession proceedings against a secure tenant for anti-social behaviour, the provisions of article 8 have been held to add nothing substantively to the requirements for a possession order under the Housing Act 1985.[118] The eviction of a disabled tenant on grounds of rent arrears pursued the legitimate aim of protecting the rights of others, and it was held to have been necessary because considerable weight had to be given to the efforts of the authorities to avoid the eviction and to the unco-operative behaviour of the tenant.[119] The service of notice to quit by a local authority in respect of the stationing of a gypsy caravan on a site was justified, because there was no unconditional right to remain.[120] The service of notice to quit by one of two joint local authority tenants, thereby terminating the tenancy rights of the other tenant, was also justified because there was no right to become the sole tenant.[121]

---

116 *R (on the application of Johns and McLellan) v Bracknell Forest DC* (2001) 33 HLR 45, QBD – presently subject to an appeal.

117 *Poplar Housing and Regeneration Community Association Ltd v Donoghue* [2001] EWCA Civ 595; [2001] 3 WLR 183, CA.

118 *Lambeth LBC v Howard* [2001] EWCA Civ 468.

119 *Marzari v Italy* (1999) 28 EHRR CD175, ECtHR. See also para 8.27.

120 *P v UK*, App No 14751/89, EComHR. See also *R (on the application of Ward) v Hillingdon LBC* [2001] EWHC Admin 91, where the decision by the local authority to issue a removal direction under section 77(1) of the Criminal Justice and Public Order Act 1994, and thus to seek eviction of a traveller from a caravan site, was held to have been justified under article 8(2).

121 *Ure v UK*, App No 28027/95, EComHR, which followed *Crawley BC v Ure* [1996] QB 13, CA.

Landlord's position

2.55 Conversely, the operation of laws giving tenants security of tenure has been held not to infringe the landlord's rights under article 8, where the landlord wished to live in the premises. The balancing of the competing interests by the national courts satisfied the requirements of the Convention.[122]

Planning and compulsory purchase

2.56 The application of planning controls against the stationing of gypsy caravans has been held to have been justified using the above principles.[123] The material factors were the limited nature of the right to respect for the home under article 8, the fact that the home had been established unlawfully, and the suitability of alternative accommodation. In another case, the requirement by a planning authority for the occupier to remove or lower a garden fence erected in breach of planning controls was justified in the interests of neighbouring occupiers.[124] The making of compulsory purchase orders against the owners of property has also been held to have been justified, because the competing interests were balanced and proper compensation was afforded.[125]

Nuisance

2.57 The interference arising from excessive dust caused by the construction work of the Limehouse Link tunnel was held to be justified, having regard to the importance of the regeneration of London's Docklands and the necessity for the road.[126] The other factors relied upon in reaching this conclusion were: the absence of health problems, the limited period of time, the applicants' failure to take steps to prevent the nuisance while it was happening, and the limited effectiveness and difficulties inherent in trying to assess compensation after the event.

122 *Velosa Barreto v Portugal* (1996) Series A No 334; [1996] EHRLR 212, ECtHR .

123 *Chapman v UK* (2001) 10 BHRC 48, ECtHR. See also *Lay v UK*, App No 13341/87, EComHR; *Mabey v UK* (1996) 22 EHRR CD 123, EComHR; *Woolhead v UK* App No 31219/96, EComHR; *Webb v UK* App No 31006/96, EComHR; *Lee v UK*, ECtHR, and the other cases reported with *Chapman*, above.

124 *Hamer v Netherlands* App No 48857/99, ECtHR.

125 *Howard v UK* (1985) 9 EHRR 116, EComHR; *Maggiuli v UK* App No 12736/87, EComHR.

126 *Khatun v UK* (1998) 26 EHRR CD 212, EComHR. Contrast *Marcic*, note 90, above.

Article 1, Protocol No 1 – Protection of property

Introduction

Every natural or legal person is entitled to the peaceful enjoyment of his possessions. No one shall be deprived of his possessions except in the public interest and subject to the conditions provided for by law and by the general principles of international law.

The preceding provisions shall not, however, in any way impair the right of a State to enforce such laws as it deems necessary to control the use of property in accordance with the general interest or to secure the payment of taxes or other contributions or penalties.

3.1   This chapter explains the scope of article 1, Protocol 1,[1] what constitutes interference with this Convention right, and whether such interference can be justified. Article 1/1 protects the enjoyment of possessions. This right has routinely been relied on by landlords and other property owners, though it is also capable of applying to tenancies and other forms of occupier's interest.

Possessions

3.2   The term possessions has an autonomous meaning[2] under the Convention, so that the meaning of this term in domestic law is not decisive. Indeed, possessions has a wider meaning than the English wording would suggest, because the equivalent term in the French text[3] demonstrates that a broad range of interests was intended to be protected.[4]

Property, contracts and licences

3.3   All forms of real and other property,[5] including leases,[6] are covered. Beyond what might ordinarily be considered to be property in English law, possessions also include contractual rights,[7] and other interests such as a liquor licence.[8] Accordingly, contractual licences to occupy land ought to be included.

1   For convenience this is referred to as article 1/1 throughout this book.
2   See generally para 6.5, below.
3   '*Biens*'.
4   See *Wiggins v UK* (1978) 13 DR 40, EComHR.
5   Corporeal and incorporeal interests in property are included.
6   See *Mellacher v Austria* (1989) Series A No 169; 12 EHRR 391, ECtHR.
7   See, for example, *Association of General Practitioners v Denmark* (1989) 62 DR 226, EComHR.
8   *Tre Traktörer Aktiebolag v Sweden* (1984) Series A No 159; 13 EHRR 309, ECtHR.

Requirement for legal right

3.4 An occupier who has no legal rights of their own, however, has no protection under this provision, so that the same-sex partner of a deceased secure tenant, having no independent interest and no right to succeed to the tenancy, could not rely on article 1/1.[9] Similarly, a soldier who occupied military lodgings, under an 'allocation form' and without any written agreement, was held not to have any interest protected by article 1/1, on the ground that the right to live in a particular property not owned by him did not constitute a possession.[10]

Legitimate expectations

3.5 In some cases, the concept of possessions has been enlarged to include apparent rights and claims which are nothing more than the legitimate expectation of obtaining effective enjoyment of a property right.[11] A planning permission, on the strength of which a person purchased land, but which was later held by a national court to have been a nullity from the beginning, was held by the ECtHR to be a component part of the property in question. Thus, until the national court's judgment was given, the purchaser had a legitimate expectation of being able to carry out the proposed development, and the national court's decision did therefore amount to an interference.[12] In another case, a claim for compensation in tort, in respect of which there was a legitimate expectation that the claim would be determined in accordance with the national law, and under which the claim arose immediately after the applicant had suffered damage, was held to be an asset protected by article 1/1.[13]

---

9 *S v UK* (1986) 47 DR 274, EComHR.

10 *JLS v Spain* App No 41917/98, ECtHR. See also *Durini v Italy* (1994) 76–B DR 76, EComHR, where the female dependents of a beneficiary under a will were held to have no possession in relation to the occupation of a property, which passed on his death under the terms of the will to another male beneficiary.

11 *Potocka v Poland* App No 33776/96, ECtHR; but see also para 3.7, below, as to restitution.

12 *Pine Valley Developments Ltd v Ireland* (1991) Series A No 222; 14 EHRR 319, ECtHR.

13 *Pressos Compania Naviera SA v Belgium* (1995) Series A No 332; 21 EHRR 301, ECtHR.

No right to acquire possessions[14]

3.6   Article 1/1 protects only a person's existing possessions, and does not guarantee the right to acquire possessions.[15] There was no right to purchase housing within a state-supported housing co-operative scheme.[16] Similarly, a claim for damages arising from an attempt to acquire shares in a housing corporation did not engage article 1/1.[17]

No right to restitution of possessions

3.7   There is no guarantee of a right, under article 1/1, to the restitution of possessions,[18] though it is not entirely easy to reconcile this with the recognition which is given to the protection of legitimate expectations.[19] Possessions do not, however, include the hope of recognition of a former property right which has not been susceptible of effective exercise for a long period of time.[20]

The structure of article 1/1

3.8   The structure of article 1/1 is somewhat complicated. It comprises three connected parts. The general rule, which informs the rest, is contained in the first sentence, and guarantees the peaceful enjoyment of property. The second rule, contained in the second sentence, protects against the deprivation of possessions and makes it subject to certain conditions. The third rule, contained in the second paragraph, recognises that states are entitled, among other things, to control the use of property in accordance with the general interest. Deprivation and control are particular instances of interference with

---

14   Compare the position under article 8, above, which accords no general right to acquire a home.
15   *Marckx v Belgium* (1979) Series A No 31; 2 EHRR 330, para 50, ECtHR. See also *Van der Mussele v Belgium* (1983) Series A no 70; 6 EHRR 163, para 48, ECtHR.
16   *Rudzinska v Poland* App No 45223/99, ECtHR.
17   *Jacq v Finland* App No 22470/95, EComHR.
18   *Jonas v Czech Republic* App No 23063/93, EComHR; *Nohejl v Czech Republic* App No 23889/93, EComHR.
19   *Potocka v Poland* App No 33776/96, ECtHR.
20   *Panikian v Bulgaria* App No 29583/96, EComHR; *Potocka v Poland*, see note 11 above.

the enjoyment of property, so that the second and third rules have to be interpreted in the light of the first.[21]

Interference

3.9 It follows from the above that there are three bases of protection: freedom from interference with peaceful enjoyment of possessions, freedom from deprivation of possessions, and freedom from control over the use of possessions.[22] It is accordingly possible for there to be an interference with the right under article 1/1 which is not either a deprivation or a control of property.[23]

Deprivation

3.10 A deprivation of property occurs when the owner's rights are extinguished. Leasehold enfranchisement legislation contained in the Leasehold Reform Act 1967, and which effected a compulsory transfer of title, gave rise to the deprivation of possessions.[24] Compulsory purchase orders are another example.[25] Other cases have included expropriation[26] and nationalisation.[27]

Control of use

3.11 A control over the use of possessions may take a wide variety of forms. Commonly, such control affects a landlord's freedom to deal with property, though issues may also arise in relation to other owners and

---

21 See, for example, *Former King of Greece v Greece* App No 25701/94, 23 November 2000.
22 See *Sporrong and Lönnroth v Sweden* (1982) Series A No 52; 5 EHRR 35, ECtHR.
23 See, for example, *Stran Greek Refineries and Stratis Andreadis v Greece* (1994) Series A No 301–B; 19 EHRR 293, ECtHR, where the government had introduced legislation to nullify an arbitral award against it. See also *Papamichalopoulos v Greece* (1993) Series A No 260–B; 16 EHRR 440, ECtHR, where there were difficulties identifying the nature of the interference.
24 *James v UK* (1986) Series A No 98; 8 EHRR 123, ECtHR.
25 *X v UK* (1970) 3 CD 72, EComHR; *Maggiulli v UK* App No 12736/87, EComHR. Both are examples of Compulsory Purchase Orders (CPOs) under Housing Act 1957 powers. See also *Howard v UK* (1985) 9 EHRR 116, EComHR, where the overlap between article 1/1 and article 8 was noted.
26 See, for example, *Papachelas v Greece* (1999) 30 EHRR 923, ECtHR.
27 See, for example, *Lithgow v UK* (1986) Series A No 102; 8 EHRR 329, ECtHR.

tenants. In *Mellacher v Austria*,[28] rent control legislation was held to be such an interference.[29] Other controls affecting private landlords have been local authority restrictions on the selection of tenants,[30] providing security of tenure to tenants,[31] and local authority control orders.[32] Controls affecting owners have included provisions for majority voting between joint owners about a possible sale,[33] island entry restrictions which reduced the number of possible purchasers,[34] and the compulsory transfer of hunting rights enabling hunting to take place on land regardless of an owner's personal views.[35] A contractual clause requiring a tenant to make contributions towards a tenants' union was held not to be inconsistent with article 1/1.[36] No interference was involved in relation to an authority's informal and internal discussions relating to plans to build new roads which affected the applicant's attempts to sell his house.[37]

Justification

General requirements

3.12   Although, as interpreted by the ECtHR, article 1/1 covers three different forms of interference with property, the ECtHR's approach to the issue of justification has tended to follow a common path.[38] The key question in each case is whether the interference achieves a 'fair balance' between the rights of the victim and the general interest,

28 (1989) Series A No 169; 12 EHRR 391, ECtHR.
29 See also *Terra Woningen BV v Netherlands* App No 20641/92, EComHR.
30 *CB BV and OH BV v Netherlands* App No 11452/85, EComHR; *Linden v Sweden* App No 12836/87, EComHR.
31 *Zammit v Malta* App No 16756/90, EComHR; *Reuter v Germany* App No 32009/96, EComHR.
32 *Orakpo v UK* App Nos 18592–3/91, EComHR.
33 *Thorsteinsson and Morthens v Iceland* App No 30323/96, EComHR.
34 *Walker-Bow v UK* App No 17176/90, EComHR.
35 *Chassagnou v France* (1999) 29 EHRR 615, ECtHR.
36 *Langborger v Sweden* (1989) Series A No 155; 12 EHRR 416, ECtHR; *Cunningham v Sweden* App No 11914/86, EComHR; *J and EH v Sweden* App No 13347/87, EComHR.
37 *Pincock v UK* App No 14265/88, EComHR.
38 An interference which does not affect the 'very essence' of the victim's right under article 1/1 is, however, easier to justify: see, for example, *Linden v Sweden* App No 12836/87, EComHR. As to the comparative degrees of interference, see also *Zammit v Malta*, above.

which involves proportionality.[39] The tendency, however, has been to accord the state a wide margin of appreciation,[40] particularly where complex and difficult issues are at stake.[41]

3.13   Similar to article 8, questions also arise in this context about whether interferences are in accordance with the conditions required by law, and whether they pursue a legitimate aim.[42] The requirement for the rule of law, in relation to article 1/1, not only arises from the express terms of the second and third sentences which refer to the requirements and enforcement of laws, but also because the ECtHR has held that the rule of law is inherent in all the articles of the Convention.[43] It is not necessary, though, that the law should provide a solution to every specific problem, and a wide statutory discretion given to a local authority was held to satisfy the test of a 'law' because there was guidance as to the exercise of the discretion, and the authority's decisions were subject to administrative appeal.[44]

Leasehold enfranchisement

3.14   In *James v UK*,[45] the trustees of the Duke of Westminster complained about the effect of giving long-leaseholders the right to enfranchisement under the Leasehold Reform Act 1967. The ECtHR held that article 1/1 applied, because there was a deprivation of the landlord's interest, but that this was justified as a matter of social policy. The elimination of social injustice by leasehold reform legislation was a legitimate aim, and fell within the state's margin of appreciation. The method of reform was not inappropriate or disproportionate, and it was not unreasonable to restrict the right of enfranchisement to less valuable properties, because these were perceived to be the cases of greatest hardship.

---

39   *Sporrong and Lönnroth* at note 22 above; *Stran Greek Refineries* at note 23 above; see further para 6.23, below.

40   *Former King of Greece v Greece* App No 25701/94, judgment 23 November 2000, ECtHR.

41   See, for example, *Sporrong and Lönnroth*, above; though even here there was held to have been an unjustified interference.

42   For an explanation of these requirements, see paras 2.44 to 2.46, above. For the overlap between articles 8 and 1/1 see *Howard v UK* (1985) 9 EHRR 116, EComHR.

43   *Amuur v France* (1996) 22 EHRR 533, ECtHR.

44   *Linden v Sweden* App No 12836/87, EComHR.

45   (1986) Series A No 98; 8 EHRR 123, ECtHR.

Rent control

3.15   The width of the state's margin of appreciation is particularly striking where the interference falls short of outright deprivation of property. In *Mellacher v Austria*,[46] the ECtHR held that in the implementation of social and economic policies, especially in the field of housing, the legislature must have a wide margin of appreciation, both in relation to the existence of a problem of public concern which warranted intervention, and in relation to the choice of the detailed provisions to implement that intervention. Accordingly, statutory rent control provisions were held to be justified, even though these affected existing contracts.[47]

Compensation

3.16   Compensation is a central issue in relation to justification, particularly where the deprivation of property is concerned. The taking of property without payment of compensation of an amount reasonably related to its value will normally constitute a disproportionate interference which would not be justified.[48] In practical terms, the absence of any compensation will require a convincing explanation from the state; and the lack of compensation has been held to upset the fair balance, to the detriment of victims, between the protection of property and the requirements of public interest.[49] On the other hand, article 1/1 falls short of a guarantee of full compensation in all circumstances, because legitimate objectives of the public interest may call for an amount which is less than full market value.[50] An inflexible system of assessing the amount of compensation, which took no account of the diversity of factual situations, was held though to be unjustified because the victims had to carry a particular and excessive burden.[51]

Compulsory purchase

3.17   The application of these principles is demonstrated by *Howard v UK*,[52] where the applicants had occupied their property for over fifty years.

---

46   (1989) Series A No 169; 12 EHRR 391, ECtHR.
47   See also *Terra Woningen BV v Netherlands* App No 20641/92, EComHR.
48   *James v UK* see note 24 above.
49   *Former King of Greece v Greece*, note 21 above, concerning the deprivation of royal lands.
50   *Papachelas v Greece* (1999) 30 EHRR 923, ECtHR.
51   Ibid.
52   (1985) 9 EHRR 116, EComHR.

They objected to a compulsory purchase order being made by the local authority for the purposes of improving and encouraging the development of new housing. The interference was held to be justified. The inspector had considered the respective effects of making or not making the order. The personal connection of the applicants with the property, together with their needs, were offset by the offer of suitable alternative accommodation in the vicinity, the entitlement to full compensation, and the detrimental effect on the local authority's scheme if the applicants were permitted to remain in their house.

3.18   In *X v UK*,[53] the applicant argued that a compulsory purchase order under the provisions of the Housing Act 1957, arising from unfitness of the applicant's properties, was a violation of article 1/1 because of inadequate compensation. The applicant complained that compensation was assessed on the basis of the site value alone. The application was rejected, because the Commission held that the houses had no value as dwelling-houses since they were unfit for human habitation, and the compensation was thus adequate.[54] In another case, a compulsory purchase order arising from disrepair was held to have been justified, because the landlord's difficulties in obtaining possession orders against his tenants (in the absence of which he could not carry out the necessary works) had been taken into account.[55]

Excessive delay

3.19   There has been a large number of cases concerning Italy, where landlords have successfully challenged, under article 1/1, long delays of very many years in enforcing possession orders, notwithstanding the wide margin of appreciation.[56] On the other hand, a delay of 18 months was held not to be excessive, particularly where the landlord had acquired the property knowing that there was tenant who was unwilling to move.[57]

---

53 4 February 1970.

54 See also *Pincock v UK* App No 14265/88, EComHR, where it was held that the terms for compensation meant that a Compulsory Purchase Order was justified, and that it was permissible under article 1/1 to give more compensation to occupiers than non-occupiers.

55 *Maggiuli v UK* App No 12736/87, EComHR.

56 See, for example, *Immobiliari Saffi v Italy* (1999) 30 EHRR 756, ECtHR – a delay in total of over eleven years. See also *GL v Italy* App No 22671/93, EComHR, where there was a delay of over seven years.

57 *Riboli v Italy* App No 31109/96, EComHR. See also *Caselli v Italy* App No 36679/97, EComHR, where a delay of up to two years was held not to be excessive.

Other examples

3.20   Compelling small landowners to transfer hunting rights over their land, so that others could make use of them in a way which was wholly incompatible with their beliefs, imposed a disproportionate burden on them which was not justified.[58]

3.21   The enforcement of planning controls against the stationing of gypsy caravans has been held to be justified for the purposes of article 1/1, in the same way as under article 8.[59]

3.22   The restriction by a local authority of future residence permits to cases of urgent housing need was held to be justified in view of a housing shortage.[60]

3.23   A victim's awareness of the circumstances constituting the interference, at the time of acquisition of the property, is likely to be a material factor helping to justify the interference.[61] Similarly, the fact that a person had freely entered into a contractual obligation affecting their property rights was held to be material.[62] In *Ure v UK*,[63] the Commission held that any interference which could be established by the applicant as a result of the other joint tenant of a local authority serving notice to quit a periodic tenancy was justified, having regard to the fact that it was clear at the outset of the tenancy that neither of them could claim the right to be the sole tenant, and because the housing authority had fairly considered the changed circumstances of the applicant who had obtained alternative accommodation.

3.24   It has been held that a judicial decision as to who is the true owner of property, in a case concerning an issue of adverse possession, can never be an unjustified state interference, because it is the very function of the courts to determine disputes.[64]

---

58   *Chassagnou v France* (1999) 29 EHRR 615, ECtHR.
59   *Chapman v UK* (2001) 10 BHRC 48, ECtHR. See also *Lay v UK* App No 13341/87, EComHR; *Mabey v UK* (1996) 22 EHRR CD 123, EComHR; *Woolhead v UK* App No 31219/96, EComHR; *Webb v UK* App No 31006/96, EComHR; *Lee v UK*, ECtHR, and the other cases reported with *Chapman*, above.
60   *CB BV and OH BV v Netherlands* App No 11452/85, EComHR.
61   *Linden v Sweden* App No 12836/87, EComHR; *Walker-Bow v UK* App No 17176/90, EComHR.
62   *J and EH v Sweden* App No 13347/87, EComHR.
63   App No 28027/95, EComHR, which followed from *Crawley BC v Ure* [1996] QB 13, CA.
64   *Uthke v Poland* App No 48684/99, ECtHR.

CHAPTER 4

Article 6 – Right to a fair trial

continued

Introduction

(1) In the determination of his civil rights and obligations or of any criminal charge against him, everyone is entitled to a fair and public hearing within a reasonable time by an independent and impartial tribunal established by law. Judgment shall be pronounced publicly but the press and public may be excluded from all or part of the trial in the interest of morals, public order or national security in a democratic society, where the interests of juveniles or the protection of the private life of the parties so require, or to the extent strictly necessary in the opinion of the court in special circumstances where publicity would prejudice the interests of justice.

4.1   This chapter explains the scope and requirements of article 6, and its application to administrative decision-making. Article 6 is concerned with the procedural guarantees associated with the concept of a fair trial, in distinction to the substantive rights considered above and which are protected by articles 8 and 1/1. Even though the focus of article 6 is purely procedural, it has proved to be one of the most important Convention rights in practical terms. It is one of the most frequently-cited provisions, and has produced a considerable body of case-law. As the ECtHR has repeatedly stated, the right to a fair trial is one of the 'fundamental principles of any democratic society within the meaning of the Convention',[1] and it is not to be interpreted restrictively.

4.2   Article 6(1) provides for the right to a fair and public hearing, within a reasonable time, and before an independent and impartial tribunal established by law. This right arises in respect of the determination of a person's civil rights and obligations, or of any criminal charge. Article 6(2) embodies the presumption of innocence in criminal cases, and article 6(3) provides for certain other minimum rights for those charged with criminal offences. Those aspects of housing which are concerned with criminal law are outside the scope of this book, and the reader should refer elsewhere for these.[2]

---

1   See, for example, *Sutter v Switzerland* (1984) Series A No 74; 6 EHRR 272, para 26, ECtHR.
2   See, for example, *European Human Rights Law*, Starmer (LAG, 2000); *Human Rights Act 1998: A practitioner's guide*, Baker, ed, (Sweet & Maxwell, 1998), chap 4.

Civil rights and obligations

4.3   The phrase 'civil rights and obligations' has an autonomous mean-ing[3] within the Convention, and means rights and obligations which arise in private law.[4] This has been approached on a case by case basis, and the ECtHR has not developed a general definition. This has in-volved looking at the nature, or 'character', of the right or obligation, rather than the manner in which it is determined. This has not proved problematic in respect of legal relations between private persons, but has proved more difficult in respect of the relations between a private person and the state. In *Stran Greek Refineries and Stratis Andreadis v Greece*, the ECtHR summarised the position in this way:[5]

> Article 6(1) applies irrespective of the status of the parties, of the nature of the legislation which governs the manner in which the dispute is to be determined and of the character of the authority which has jurisdiction in the matter; it is enough that the outcome of the proceedings should be decisive for private rights and obligations.

Examples

4.4   Several areas in which the state has relations with private persons have been held to give rise to civil rights and obligations. These include refusal of permission to occupy residential premises,[6] expropriation of land,[7] planning decisions,[8] regulation and licensing decisions,[9] and rights to compensation.[10] The ECtHR has gone as far as recognising certain social security rights within this category.[11] In contrast, proceedings aimed at changing a zoning plan did not involve a determination of civil rights.[12]

3   As to the meaning of this generally, see below, para 6.5.

4   *König v Federal Republic of Germany* (1978) Series A No 27; 2 EHRR 170, para 95, ECtHR.

5   (1994) Series A No 301–B; 19 EHRR 293, para 39, ECtHR. See also *R (on the application of Holding and Barnes plc) v Secretary of State for the Environment, Transport and the Regions* [2001] UKHL 23; [2001] 2 WLR 1389.

6   *Gillow v UK* (1986) Series A No 109; 11 EHRR 335, ECtHR.

7   *Sporrong and Lönnroth v Sweden* (1982) Series A No 52; 5 EHRR 35, ECtHR.

8   *Bryan v UK* (1995) Series A No 335–A; 21 EHRR 342, ECtHR.

9   *Tre Traktorer Aktiebolag v Sweden* (1989) Series A No 159; 13 EHRR 309, ECtHR.

10   *Editions Périscope v France* (1992) Series A No 234–B; 14 EHRR 597, ECtHR. See also *Stran Greek Refineries and Stratis Andreadis v Greece* (1994) Series A No 301–B; 19 EHRR 293, ECtHR.

11   See, for example, *Massa v Italy* (1993) Series A No 265–B; 18 EHRR 266, ECtHR.

12   *Inhabitants of Ruigoord v Netherlands*, App No 14443/88, EComHR. See also *Jacobsson v Sweden*, App No 11309/84, EComHR.

Public/private law analogy

4.5   An analogy may be drawn with the public/private law distinction which has developed in domestic law; but, for the purposes of Convention law, it has been emphasised that the test is in respect of the 'substantive contents and effects of the right – and not its legal classification under the domestic law of the State concerned'.[13]

Determinations

4.6   The application of article 6(1) pre-supposes a properly arguable dispute which is the subject-matter of a determination. In *James v UK*, this was explained in the following way:[14]

> Article 6(1) extends only to 'contestations' (disputes) over (civil) 'rights and obligations' which can be said, at least on arguable grounds, to be recognised under domestic law: it does not in itself guarantee any particular content for (civil) 'rights and obligations' in the substantive law of the Contracting States.

Requirement for an arguable claim

4.7   An applicant must therefore identify at least an arguable claim under domestic law. Thus, in *Powell and Rayner v UK*,[15] the applicants complained about excessive noise levels suffered in their properties near Heathrow Airport. The ECtHR held that there was no jurisdiction to entertain a complaint under article 6(1), because the complaint was directed against the limitation of domestic liability under the Civil Aviation Act 1982. The court reasoned:[16]

> ... the effect of [the statutory provisions] is to exclude liability in nuisance with regard to the flight of aircraft in certain circumstances, with the result that the applicants cannot claim to have a substantive right under English law to obtain relief for exposure to aircraft noise in those circumstances. To this extent there is no 'civil right' recognised under domestic law to attract the application of article 6(1).

13   *Konig v Germany* (1978) Series A No 27; 2 EHRR 170, ECtHR.

14   (1986) Series A No 98; 8 EHRR 123, para 81, ECtHR. In *St Brice v Southwark LBC* [2001] EWCA Civ 1138; (2001) *Times* 6 August, CA, it was held that the determination of the right to possession was made at the time of the order and not when the landlord sought to enforce the order by warrant.

15   (1990) Series A No 172; 12 EHRR 355, ECtHR.

16   At para 36 of the judgment.

Restraint of state immunity

4.8   The state does not, however, enjoy unlimited scope to remove arguments of civil liability from the jurisdiction of the courts.[17] In *Fayed v UK*, the ECtHR observed:[18]

> ... it would not be consistent with the rule of law in a democratic society or with the basic principle underlying article 6(1) – namely that civil claims must be capable of being submitted to a judge for adjudication – if, for example, a State could, without restraint or control by the Convention enforcement bodies, remove from the jurisdiction of the courts a whole range of civil claims or confer immunities from civil liability on large groups or categories of persons.

Broad meaning of 'dispute'

4.9   A dispute may involve questions of fact as well as law, and may concern not only the existence of a right but also its scope and manner of enjoyment. It must, however, be genuine and of a serious nature.[19]

Right of access to a court, and legal aid

4.10   Article 6(1) has been interpreted in a purposive manner to include the right to a court, including the right of access in order to instigate proceedings.[20] Using this approach, it has been held, for example, that an applicant had effectively been denied access to a court for the purpose of obtaining a judicial separation, because legal representation was required and the applicant could neither afford it nor obtain legal aid.[21] This decision does not, however, establish a general right to legal aid in civil cases, though it should assist in cases of particular difficulty. Various factors are relevant, including the ability of the person to put their case effectively, the relative importance of the issues raised, other avenues of redress, and the existence of reasonable prospects of success. The state may, however, be compelled to provide for the assistance of a lawyer when such assistance is indispensable for effective access to the court, either because legal representation is

17 See further, right of access to a court, at para 4.10 below.
18 (1994) Series A No 294–B; 18 EHRR 393, para 65, ECtHR.
19 *Benthem v Netherlands* (1985) 8 EHRR 1, ECtHR.
20 *Golder v UK* (1975) Series A No 18; 1 EHRR 524, ECtHR.
21 *Airey v Ireland* (1979) Series A No 32; 2 EHRR 305, ECtHR.

compulsory or by reason of the complexity of the procedure or substance of the case.[22] On the particular facts, it has been held, in relation to a case concerning disrepair and the tenants' legal status, that the absence of legal representation before the Court of Appeal had not infringed the right under article 6(1).[23]

Public policy immunities

4.11   The right of access to a court has been used in order to challenge successfully the use of public policy arguments aimed at establishing immunity for public authorities. Thus, in *Osman v UK*,[24] it was held that the right under article 6(1) had been violated when the Court of Appeal had struck out a claim in negligence against the police on public policy grounds without properly considering the factual merits of the claim.[25] The standing of this decision, however, in relation to the particular case of negligence claims, appears now to be degraded, because most recently in *Z v UK*[26] the majority of the ECtHR declined to follow it and appeared to indicate that the earlier decision had been incorrect.

Enforcement of court orders

4.12   Included within the right of access to a court is the right of a litigant to the enforcement of a judgment.[27] Under this principle, enforcement cannot be unduly delayed. In a number of cases, landlords have successfully complained about the long delays of several years in the implementation of possession orders.[28]

Qualified right only

4.13   The right of access to a court is not an absolute right, and it is permissible for the state to regulate and limit the right, according to the needs and resources of the community and of individuals.[29] In this,

---

22   *K and T v Finland*, App No 25702/94, EComHR.
23   *Smith and Smith v UK* App No 49167/99, ECtHR.
24   (2000) 29 EHRR 245, ECtHR.
25   See, in consequence, *Barrett v Enfield LBC* [1999] 3 WLR 79, HL, and *Phelps v Hillingdon LBC* [2000] 3 WLR 776, HL.
26   10 May 2001, para 100, ECtHR.
27   *Hornsby v Greece* RJD 1997–II 510; 24 EHRR 250, para 40, ECtHR.
28   See, for example, *Immobiliare Saffi v Italy* (2000) 30 EHRR 756, ECtHR; *Palumbo v Italy* App No 15919/89, ECtHR.
29   *Lithgow v UK* (1986) Series A No 102; 8 EHRR 329, para 194, ECtHR.

states enjoy a margin of appreciation, but they are not permitted to impair 'the very essence of the right'; and any limitation must be justified by demonstrating a legitimate aim and a reasonable relationship of proportionality between the means employed and the aim sought to be achieved.[30]

No entitlement to an effective remedy

4.14   While article 6(1) regulates the form and conduct of proceedings relating to rights and obligations which are recognised in domestic law, it falls short of requiring the state to provide an effective remedy.[31]

Fair hearing

4.15   The substantive requirements of a fair hearing fall into two broad categories. These are, first, the specific requirements imposed by article 6(1), namely the right to a hearing before an independent and impartial tribunal established by law, a qualified right to a public hearing, the right to public pronouncement of judgment, and the right to a hearing (including judgment) within a reasonable time.[32] Second, there are general requirements implicit in the notion of a fair trial.[33]

General requirements

4.16   The general requirements of fairness are open-ended, though three key elements can be identified. These are: the principle of 'equality of arms',[34] a judicial process,[35] and the need for a reasoned decision.[36] The first of these requires a balance to be maintained between the

---

30   Ibid. See also *Stubbings v UK* (1997) 23 EHRR 213, ECtHR, where the time-barring of claims under the Limitation Act 1980 was held to be justified.

31   *H v Belgium* (1987) Series A No 127; 10 EHRR 339, ECtHR. The right to an effective remedy is protected instead by article 13, which has not been given effect under the Human Rights Act 1998.

32   See below, para 4.17 and following.

33   Similarly, the 'overriding objective' under Civil Procedure Rules (CPR) Pt 1 requires civil courts to ensure, so far as practicable, that a case is dealt with fairly: CPR 1.1(2)(d).

34   *Dombo Beheer BV v Netherlands* (1993) Series A No 274; 18 EHRR 213, ECtHR.

35   *Ruiz-Mateos v Spain* (1993) Series A No 262; 16 EHRR 505, ECtHR.

36   *Hadjianastassiou v Greece* (1992) Series A No 252–A; 16 EHRR 219, ECtHR.

parties, so that each party must be afforded a reasonable opportunity to present their case, including evidence, without substantial disadvantage relative to the opposing party.[37] Similarly, a judicial process requires each party to have knowledge of, and the opportunity to comment upon, the case of the opposing party.

Independent and impartial tribunal, established by law

4.17 Article 6(1) requires an independent and impartial tribunal established by law. The term 'tribunal' denotes a judicial function, whose decisions have the force of law.[38] 'Established by law' means that the tribunal cannot depend for its existence and operation merely on the discretion of the executive.[39] A body which also possesses administrative functions may nonetheless be a tribunal for these purposes.[40]

Independence

4.18 The tribunal must be independent of the executive and the parties. In determining independence, the following are relevant factors: the manner and duration of the appointment of the tribunal members; the existence of guarantees against outside pressures; and, whether the body presents the appearance of independence.[41]

Impartiality

4.19 Impartiality overlaps with independence, but goes further. It is concerned with the absence of prejudice or bias.[42] There are two, alternative elements to this which the tribunal must satisfy: a subjective test (ie, endeavouring to ascertain the personal conviction of a given judge in a given case) and an objective test (ie, determining whether the judge offered guarantees sufficient to exclude any legitimate doubt

---

37 Similarly, the 'overriding objective' under CPR Pt 1 requires civil courts to ensure, so far as practicable, that the parties are on an equal footing.
38 *Benthem v Netherlands* (1985) Series A No 97; 8 EHRR 1, ECtHR.
39 *Zand v Austria* (1978) 15 DR 70, EComHR.
40 *Campbell and Fell v UK* (1984) Series A No 80; 7 EHRR 165, paras 33 and 81, ECtHR.
41 Ibid.
42 *Piersack v Belgium* (1982) Series A No 53; 5 EHRR 169, ECtHR.

in this respect).[43] There is a presumption of impartiality,[44] and in practice the evidential burden of establishing subjective bias has been very difficult to overcome. In contrast, the objective test, based as it is on a legitimate doubt, has been much easier for applicants to satisfy.[45] The purpose of this test is to maintain public confidence in the courts, and appearances as well as substance are relevant. In deciding whether there is a legitimate reason to fear that a court lacks impartiality, the parties' opinion is important but not decisive: what is decisive is whether a party's fear can be regarded as being objectively justified.[46] The use of an expert belonging to the staff of a government ministry, in a dispute between the owner of land and the authorities over environmental pollution, was held not to violate this aspect of article 6(1).[47] The mere fact that the expert was employed by the same administrative authority which was involved in the case did not justify the fear that the expert was unable to act with proper neutrality, and it has been held that a contrary conclusion would place unacceptable limits on the possibility of obtaining expert advice.[48]

Composite approach

4.20   Even if a tribunal in itself lacks any of the elements required by article 6(1),[49] it is sufficient if the applicant has access to an independent judicial body with full jurisdictional control over the prior procedure, so that compositely the entire process provides the necessary guarantees.[50] Thus the availability of judicial review and other remedies may

43   Ibid, para 30. See also *Hauschildt v Denmark* (1989) Series A No 154; 12 EHRR 266, para 46, ECtHR.

44   *Le Compte, Van Leuven and De Meyere v Belgium* (1981) Series A No 43; 4 EHRR 1, para 58, ECtHR.

45   See, for example, *Piersack*, note 42 above. *Langborger v Sweden* (1989) Series A No 155; 12 EHRR 416, ECtHR. *Demicola v Malta* (1991) Series A No 210; 14 EHRR 47, ECtHR.

46   *Padovani v Italy* (1993) Series A No 257–B, ECtHR. See *In re Medicaments and Related Classes of Goods (No 2)* (2001) *Times* 2 February, CA, as to the difference between this approach and that under the 'real danger' test in *R v Gough* [1993] AC 646, HL.

47   *Beleggings en Beheersmaatschappij Indiana BV v Netherlands* App No 21491/93, EComHR. Compare *Field v Leeds City Council* (2000) 32 HLR 618, CA.

48   *Zumtobel v Austria* (1992) Series A No 268–A; 17 EHRR 116, para 86, ECtHR. *Brandstetter v Austria* (1991) Series A No 211; 15 EHRR 378, para 44, ECtHR.

49   See below, para 4.25 onwards.

50   *Bryan v UK* (1995) Series A No 335–A; 21 EHRR 342, para 40, ECtHR. See also *Crabtree v UK* (1997) 23 EHRR CD 202, EComHR, in relation to an unsuccessful claim in respect of a fostering panel.

be sufficient to cure any original deficiency, though whether this is so requires consideration of the applicant's complaints and the context.[51]

Public hearing and judgment

4.21   Article 6(1) requires judgment to be pronounced publicly, and for the hearing to be conducted generally in public. As to the latter, the Convention itself provides for the exclusion of the press and public in certain circumstances which are capable of covering a wide range of circumstances: namely, the interests of morals, public order or national security in a democratic society; where the interests of juveniles or the private life of the parties so require; or to the extent strictly necessary in the opinion of the court in special circumstances where publicity would prejudice the interest of justice.[52] A challenge to the requirement, in rent arrears cases, for possession actions to be conducted in private was rejected.[53] The right to a public hearing may be waived in appropriate circumstances.[54]

Prompt adjudication

4.22   The requirement for a hearing within a reasonable time has generated a very considerable number of applications under the Convention.[55] Delay undermines the effectiveness and credibility of justice.[56] In *Robins v UK*,[57] the resolution of costs proceedings took over four years, and there was held to have been responsibility on the part of the authorities for about half of that period, which violated article 6(1).

---

51 See generally, *Albert and Le Compte v Belgium* (1983) Series A No 58; 5 EHRR 533, ECtHR. *W v UK* (1987) Series A No 121; 10 EHRR 29, ECtHR. *Zumtobel v Austria* (1993) Series A No 268–A; 17 EHRR 116, ECtHR.

52 For the general operation of these provisions, and the finding of no violation in relation to private hearings and limited release of judgments in cases involving custody of children, see *B v UK, P v UK* (2001) *Times* 15 May, ECtHR.

53 *R (on the application of Pelling) v Bow County Court* [2001] UKHRR 165, QBD.

54 *Håkansson v Sweden* (1990) Series A No 171; 13 EHRR 1, ECtHR. See generally para 6.27 onwards.

55 See also under right of access to a court, at para 4.10 above, and cases such as *Immobiliari Saffi v Italy* (2000) 30 EHRR 756, ECtHR, in relation to undue delay in the enforcement of court orders.

56 *H v France* (1989) Series A No 162; 12 EHRR 74, ECtHR.

57 RJD 1997–V 181; 26 EHRR 527, ECtHR.

This has a clear relevance in terms of good case management,[58] and in terms of the provision and management of judicial resources.

Causes of delay

4.23   The state is responsible for delay both in particular instances, and in respect of the structure of the legal system. States have an obligation 'to organise their legal systems so as to allow the courts to comply with the requirements of article 6(1)'.[59] A failure to allocate adequate resources in response to a backlog of cases, and to deal with structural deficiencies, may engage state liability.[60] The position is different where delays result from circumstances which were not reasonably foreseeable, and the state takes reasonably prompt remedial action.[61] The state is not responsible for delay caused by the applicant.[62]

Reasonableness of delay

4.24   The reasonableness of any delay depends on all the circumstances, and there is no absolute period. Relevant factors include the complexity of the factual or legal issues, the conduct of the applicant and the authorities, and what was at stake for the applicant.[63] The state will be expected to show 'particular diligence' in cases which are critical to the applicant and have a 'particular quality of irreversibility',[64] which might well include some cases concerning occupation of the home. On the other hand, in *Tennenbaum v Sweden*,[65] a delay of over 3 years in resolving a dispute over an application for housing assistance, under which the applicant secured temporary accommodation but not a living allowance, was held not to have been excessive in all the circumstances, but the applicant had not demonstrated any particular need for speed. In *Mittermaier v Sweden*,[66] a delay of seven years in determining rent review proceedings was held not to be excessive,

---

58 Similarly, the 'overriding objective' under CPR Pt 1 requires civil courts to ensure, so far as practicable, that a case is dealt with expeditiously.

59 *Zimmerman and Steiner v Switzerland* (1983) Series A No 66; 6 EHRR 17, para 29, ECtHR.

60 *Guincho v Portugal* (1984) Series A No 81; 7 EHRR 223, ECtHR.

61 *Buchholz v FRG* (1981) Series A No 42; 3 EHRR 597, para 51, ECtHR.

62 See, for example, *Mittermaier v Sweden* App No 39493/98, ECtHR.

63 *Zimmerman*, at note 59 above.

64 *H v UK* (1987) Series A No 120; 10 EHRR 95, ECtHR.

65 App No 26909/95, EComHR.

66 See note 62 above.

because the delays were the inevitable result of the tenant's own conduct in availing himself of opportunities to take procedural action, by presenting new claims, lodging appeals, changing counsel, and requesting numerous extensions of time.

Administrative decision-making

4.25   In the context of administrative decision-making, the right to a fair hearing is not violated merely because the adjudicating body does not in itself satisfy the requirements of article 6(1). Those requirements can be met if the body is subject to control by a judicial body with full jurisdiction and which does provide the necessary guarantees.[67]

Planning cases

4.26   In *Bryan v UK*,[68] it was held that although a statutory appeal against a planning decision was restricted to points of law, and was thus not capable of embracing all aspects of the planning inspector's decision, the limited jurisdiction of the national courts nonetheless provided sufficient compliance with article 6(1).[69] A composite approach was taken to the decision-making process as a whole. The ECtHR stated:

> ... in assessing the sufficiency of the review available to [the applicant], it is necessary to have regard to matters such as the subject matter of the decision appealed against, the manner in which that decision was arrived at, and the content of the dispute, including the desired or actual grounds of appeal.

4.27   Similarly, the power of the secretary of state to take over responsibility for determining certain planning applications and appeals, although he could not be considered to be independent and impartial, has been held nonetheless to comply with article 6(1) because the powers of the courts on judicial review were sufficient to provide the necessary guarantees.[70]

67   *Albert and Le Compte v Belgium* (1983) Series A No 58; 5 EHRR 533, para 29, ECtHR. *Bryan v UK* (1995) Series A No 335–A; 21 EHRR 342, para 40, ECtHR.

68   See note 67 above.

69   The same conclusion was reached in *Chapman v UK* (2001) 10 BHRC 48, ECtHR.

70   *R (on the application of Holding and Barnes plc) v Secretary of State for the Environment, Transport and the Regions* [2001] UKHL 23; [2001] 2 WLR 1389. A particular factor in this decision was that questions of planning policy were preeminently ones for the executive rather than the courts.

Introductory tenancies

4.28   The statutory regime for introductory tenancies[71] has been held to be
        compatible with article 6(1). In *R (on the application of Johns) v Brack-
        nell Forest DC,*[72] the applicant sought a declaration of incompatibility
        under Human Rights Act 1998 s4, arguing that the process whereby
        local authorities were empowered to recover possession of premises
        let on an introductory tenancy was not compatible with article 6(1). It
        was held that the authority's decision to apply for a possession order
        was a determination of the tenant's civil rights for the purposes of
        article 6(1). Although the internal review was not of itself a review by
        an independent and impartial tribunal, the process of internal review
        when coupled with judicial review was a sufficient compliance with
        the right to a fair trial.

---

71   Housing Act 1996 Pt V. See further para 9.18, below.
72   (2001) 33 HLR 45, QBD. At the time of writing, this case and that of *Reigate and
     Banstead DC v Forrest* (unreported, county court) are subject to appeal, with
     judgment awaited..

Article 14 – Prohibition of discrimination

Introduction

> The enjoyment of the rights and freedoms set forth in this
> Convention shall be secured without discrimination on any ground
> such as sex, race, colour, language, religion, political or other
> opinion, national or social origin, association with a national
> minority, property, birth or other status.

5.1   This chapter explains the scope of article 14, what constitutes interference with this Convention right, and whether such interference
can be justified. The prohibition of discrimination under article 14
has an important place in the Convention, but it is important to note
that it is not free-standing.[1] Article 14 supports the other substantive
Convention rights, because it applies only in relation to 'the enjoyment of the rights and freedoms set forth in [the] Convention'. The
trigger for the application of article 14 is thus whether the facts at
issue fall within the ambit of one or more of the other Convention
provisions.[2] Where the facts fall outside the scope of the other rights
guaranteed under the Convention altogether, no question arises
under article 14.[3] It is not, however, necessary to demonstrate a violation of one of the substantive Convention rights in order to be able to
demonstrate a violation of article 14: it is sufficient for the purposes of
article 14 merely that one of the other Convention rights is applicable.[4]

Positive obligations

5.2   Although article 14 may impose positive obligations[5] on states,[6] it is
unclear what the scope of these may be.

Analogous situations

5.3   In order for there to be discrimination, it is necessary to be able to
compare the position of the applicant with that of another person or

1   Protocol 12 to the Convention does provide a free-standing prohibition against
discrimination, but the UK has not given effect to it.
2   *Rasmussen v Denmark* (1984) Series A No 87; 7 EHRR 371, para 29, ECtHR.
3   See, for example, *Marckx v Belgium* (1979) Series A No 31; 2 EHRR 330, para 50,
ECtHR.
4   See, for example, I*nze v Austria* (1987) Series A No 126; 10 EHRR 394, ECtHR.
5   See generally para 6.8 onwards.
6   The *Belgian Linguistic* case (1979–1980) Series A No 5; 1 EHRR 241, para I B 9,
ECtHR.

persons in an 'analogous situation'.[7] This involves considering 'persons in "relevantly" similar situations',[8] and it is for the applicant to demonstrate that there is such a comparison to be made. There is no analogy between a landlord and a tenant.[9] Nor is there any analogy between an introductory tenant and a secure tenant.[10]

Difference in treatment

5.4   Discrimination involves an unjustified difference of treatment between the applicant and other comparable persons.[11] The applicant must establish the difference of treatment, relative to the analogous situation which is claimed, and this should not be assumed to be straightforward where it is not obvious. Proving racism, for example, in cases of indirect discrimination has been problematic.[12] Complaints of discrimination were readily dismissed by the Commission in one case where allegations of bad faith against a local authority were rejected at trial and not pursued on appeal, where no specific examples of discriminatory conduct by the judges had been given, and where the mere fact that the applicant had been unsuccessful in his various attempts to challenge a control order and a compulsory purchase order were held not even to be sufficient to make out an 'at first sight' case of discrimination.[13]

Factual not theoretical differences

5.5   In *Cunningham v Sweden*,[14] a tenant sought to argue that, as a non-member of the tenants' union, he had been discriminated against because the union (to which the tenant was obliged to contribute financially through his rent) organised its activities in such a way that

---

7 *Van Der Mussele v Belgium* (1983) Series A No 70; 6 EHRR 163, para 46, ECtHR.
8 *Fresdin v Sweden* (1991) Series A No 192; 13 EHRR 784, para 60, ECtHR.
9 *Hutten-Czapska v Poland* App No 35104/97, ECtHR . *Palumbo v Italy* App No 15919/89, ECtHR. See also *Terra Woningen BV v Netherlands* App No 20641/92, EComHR, where there was held to be no analogy between a local authority and a private landlord dealing with environmental pollution.
10 *R (on the application of Johns) v Bracknell Forest DC* (2001) 33 HLR 45, QBD.
11 See, for example, *Abdulaziz, Cabales and Balkandali v UK* (1985) Series A No 94; 7 EHRR 471, ECtHR.
12 See *Abdulaziz* at note 12 above, para 85 of the judgment.
13 *Orakpo v UK* App Nos 18592–3/91, EComHR.
14 App 11914/86, EComHR.

they were controlled by its members. Because, however, the evidence suggested that no activities at all had been organised by the union, the allegation failed.

Identifying the reason for the difference

5.6 In *P v UK*,[15] the applicants were gypsies who were served with notice to quit their caravan pitch. They were excluded from statutory protection under the Mobile Homes Act 1983, and they claimed that this was discriminatory because other persons pursuing a nomadic lifestyle, such as seasonal workers, were not excluded. It was held, however, that the reason why the applicants were excluded from protection was not personal to them, but rather it was because of the classification of the site. Accordingly, their claim failed.

Gypsies and planning controls

5.7 Generally speaking, the Strasbourg authorities have accepted that gypsies suffer from a difference in treatment compared with house-dwellers in respect of the application of planning controls.[16] In one case, however, the Commission was not persuaded that the applicant was put at any material disadvantage by reason his status as a gypsy, or that house-dwellers generally received more favourable treatment in the provision of new housing within the green belt.[17]

Variety of grounds

5.8 Article 14 does not define exhaustively the grounds upon which any such difference of treatment will be caught.[18] The categories are wide and open-ended, though some grounds are treated more rigorously than others. Examples of differences in treatment include: gender,[19]

15 App 14751/89, EComHR, a case arising from the decision of the House of Lords in *Powell v Greenwich LBC* [1989] AC 995.

16 See, for example, *Chapman v UK* (2001) 10 BHRC 48, ECtHR.

17 *Woolhead v UK* App No 31219/96, EComHR.

18 *Rasmussen v Denmark* (1984) Series A No 87; 7 EHRR 371, para 34, ECtHR. It has been held, however, that article 14 prohibits discriminatory treatment which is based on a personal characteristic 'status', by which persons or groups are distinguishable: *Kjeldsen, Busk Madsen and Pedersen v Denmark* (1976) 1 EHRR 711, ECtHR. See also *St Brice v Southwark LBC* [2001] EWCA Civ 1138; (2001) *Times* 6 August, CA.

19 *Abdulaziz* at note 11 above.

race,[20] language,[21] religion,[22] nationality,[23] and illegitimate status of a child.[24] A geographical basis for a difference in treatment was recognised by the Commission in *Linden v Sweden*,[25] where the local authority declared a particular area to be subject to their control in respect of the grant of certain new private sector tenancies.[26]

Reasonable and objective justification

5.9 Not every difference in treatment is discriminatory. The benchmark is whether the state has shown a 'reasonable and objective justification' for the difference in treatment which has been found to exist – not only its existence, but also its scope.[27] The ECtHR explained this in the *Belgian Linguistic* case, as follows:[28]

> The existence of such a justification must be assessed in relation to the aim and effects of the measure under consideration, regard being had to the principles which normally prevail in democratic societies. A difference of treatment in the exercise of a right laid down in the Convention must not only pursue a legitimate aim: article 14 is likewise violated when it is clearly established that there is no reasonable relationship of proportionality between the means employed and the aim sought to be realised.

Margin of appreciation

5.10 In determining whether a difference in treatment can be justified under article 14, the ECtHR accordingly carries out a supervisory review, the scope and intensity of which depend on the circumstances, and allowing the state to make appropriate judgments within its margin of appreciation.[29] The scope of the margin of appreciation

20 *East African Asians* cases (1976) 3 EHRR 76, ECtHR.
21 The *Belgian Linguistic* case (1968) Series A No 6; 1 EHRR 252, ECtHR.
22 *Hoffmann v Austria* (1993) Series A No 255–C; 17 EHRR 293, ECtHR.
23 *Gaygusuz v Austria* RJD 1996–IV 1129; (1997) 23 EHRR 364, ECtHR.
24 *Marckx v Belgium* (1979) Series A No 31; 2 EHRR 330, ECtHR.
25 App No 12836/87, EComHR.
26 Contrast *R (on the application of Johns) v Bracknell Forest DC* (2001) 33 HLR 45, QBD, where it was doubted (it would seem wrongly) whether article 14 included discrimination on a geographical basis.
27 *National Union of Belgian Police v Belgium* (1975) Series A No 19; 1 EHRR 578, para 49, ECtHR.
28 See note 21 above, para 10.
29 See generally para 6.20 onwards, below.

varies according to the circumstances, the subject matter and the background. One of the relevant factors is the existence or lack of common ground between the laws of the contracting states.[30] In a number of cases to do with sexual equality, the ECtHR has adopted the approach that 'very weighty reasons' have to be put forward to justify a difference in treatment based exclusively on sex, and the margin of appreciation is accordingly narrow.[31] The same is true of differentiation based on nationality,[32] race,[33] and religion.[34]

Legitimate aims

5.11   Legitimate aims in this context have included: leaseholder enfranchisement,[35] protection of the family,[36] preferential treatment in relation to housing for those with strong attachments to an island,[37] protection of the health and rights of children,[38] and the protection of morals and rights of others.[39]

Fair balance

5.12   In the *Belgian Linguistic* case,[40] the ECtHR held that article 14 does not prohibit different treatment where this is:

> ... founded on an objective assessment of essentially different factual circumstances and which, being based on the public interest, strike a fair balance between the protection of the interests of the community and respect for the rights and freedoms safeguarded by the Convention.

---

30 *Rasmussen v Denmark* (1984) Series A No 87; 7 EHRR 371, para 40, ECtHR.
31 See *Abdulaziz* at note 11 above, para 78. *Van Raalte v Netherlands* (1997) 24 EHRR 503, para 39, ECtHR .
32 *Gaygusuz v Austria* (1996) 23 EHRR 364, para 42, ECtHR.
33 *Abdulaziz*, above, paras 84–85.
34 *Hoffmann v Austria* (1993) Series A No 255–C; 17 EHRR 293, para 36, ECtHR.
35 *James v UK* (1986) Series A No 98; 8 EHRR 123, para 76, ECtHR.
36 *S v UK* (1986) 47 DR 274, EComHR.
37 *Gillow v UK* (1986) Series A No 109; 11 EHRR 335, para 65, ECtHR.
38 *Hoffmann v Austria*, above, para 34.
39 *Sutherland v UK* (1997) 24 EHRR CD22, para 54, EComHR.
40 (1996) Series A No 6; 1 EHRR 252, para II 7.

Government tenants

5.13　The application of these principles is illustrated by *Larkos v Cyprus*,[41] where the applicant was a retired civil servant who rented his home from the government, under a 20 year lease. On expiry of the lease, the government sought to evict him. The national courts held that government tenants did not have security of tenure, and accordingly granted possession. The ECtHR, however, held that the deprivation of the applicant's home was discriminatory. The lease made no reference to the fact that the applicant was a civil servant, and made it clear that the government had rented the property under private law. On the facts, the differentiation between government tenants and private tenants did not pursue a legitimate aim, and no reasonable and objective justification had been established.

Right to buy and enfranchisement

5.14　On the other hand, in *Strunjak v Croatia*,[42] a difference in treatment between public and private sector tenants, by reason of the exclusion of the latter from the right to buy, was held to be objective and reasonable. The ECtHR recognised the legitimate interest of the owners to have their ownership protected, whereas no such private rights of ownership were involved in the case of public sector properties. It was also emphasised that the applicants had never been in any different position. Correspondingly, in *James v UK*,[43] it was held that the differences in the treatment as between different property owners under the enfranchisement provisions in the Leasehold Reform Act 1967 were justified. The social objectives involved in housing policy were such that the state enjoyed a wide margin of appreciation, and the differences in treatment were proportionate and reasonably and objectively justified, without imposing an unreasonable or disproportionate burden on the applicants.

Other examples

5.15　In *Spadea v Italy*,[44] the Court held that the suspension by legislative decree of eviction orders obtained by the applicant landlords against

---

41　(2000) 30 EHRR 597, ECtHR.
42　App No 46934/99, ECtHR.
43　(1986) Series A No 98; 8 EHRR 123, ECtHR.
44　(1995) Series A No 315–B; 21 EHRR 482, para 46, ECtHR.

their tenants was justified in circumstances of a serious housing shortage.

5.16   In planning cases, it has been held that the disadvantage caused to gypsies by the enforcement of controls against the stationing of caravans was not discriminatory.[45]

5.17   In *Chassagnou v France*,[46] a law on hunting which required small landowners to transfer their hunting rights to the community, whereas large landowners were exempted, was held to be unjustified because no convincing explanation had been given for differentiating on the basis of the size of the holding.

---

45 *Chapman v UK* (2001) 10 BHRC 48, ECtHR.
46 (1999) 29 EHRR 615, ECtHR.

CHAPTER 6

General principles

continued

Introduction

6.1 This chapter explains the relevant general principles which govern the application and interpretation of the Convention, and the remedies obtainable under it.

Victims

6.2 The concept of a victim is crucial to the operation of the Convention because, apart from states, only victims can bring proceedings under the Convention. This is also important under the Human Rights Act 1998 because the same victim test governs the ability to raise allegations under section 6, for instance, that a public authority has acted unlawfully in a way incompatible with the Convention rights. This is considered in chapter 13, below.

Interpretation generally

6.3 The Convention is an international treaty, and as such it is to be interpreted according to rules of international law set out in the Vienna Convention on the Law of Treaties 1969.[1] Article 31(1) of the Vienna Convention requires that a treaty:

> ... shall be interpreted in good faith in accordance with the ordinary meaning to be given to the terms of the treaty in their context and in the light of its object and purposes.

In appropriate cases, recourse may be had to supplementary means of interpretation. These include the preparatory or background work on a treaty,[2] similar to the use of *Hansard* in resolving a question of statutory interpretation. Such sources can be used to confirm the meaning resulting from Vienna Convention article 31, or to determine the meaning when interpretation leaves the meaning ambiguous or obscure, or when it leads to a result that is manifestly absurd or un-reasonable.[3] The ECtHR[4] has not often consulted these sources and there may be a tendency or need now to do so even less because the case-law has extensively interpreted the Convention.

---

1   Cmnd 7964.
2   The preparatory work on the Convention is published in *Collected Edition of the Travaux Préparatoires of the European Convention on Human Rights*.
3   See Vienna Convention article 32.
4   See, for example, *Lithgow v UK* (1986) Series A No 102; 8 EHRR 329, ECtHR, where the sources were considered in connection with article 1/1.

Purposive approach

6.4   In accordance with the Vienna Convention, the Strasbourg authorities adopt a purposive approach to the interpretation of the Convention. This requires the courts:

> ... to seek the interpretation that is most appropriate in order to realise the aim and achieve the object of the treaty, and not that which would restrict to the greatest possible degree the obligations undertaken by the parties.[5]

The Strasbourg authorities also insist that the Convention rights should be 'practical and effective', and not merely theoretical.[6]

Autonomous meanings

6.5   Words used in the Convention have 'autonomous meanings'. This signifies that the meaning of the words is determined by the Convention itself, and not by their meaning in national law. National law is a starting point, but it is not decisive. Examples of this include the words home,[7] possessions,[8] and law.[9]

Common standards and trends

6.6   The ECtHR looks for common standards across the states which are parties to the Convention, and will respond critically where a state is out of line.[10] Where an attempt is being made to develop the case-law into new areas, the ECtHR will also look to see whether a trend in that direction exists.[11] It may thus be relevant to consider foreign law where Convention rights are concerned.

---

5 *Wemhoff v Federal Republic of Germany* (1968) Series A No 7; 1 EHRR 55, para 8, ECtHR.
6 *Artico v Italy* (1980) Series A No 37; 3 EHRR 7, para 33, ECtHR.
7 In article 8 – see para 2.20, above.
8 In article 1/1 – see para 3.2, above.
9 In articles 6, 8 and 1/1 – see para 2.45, above.
10 See, for example, *Tyrer v UK* (1978) Series A No 26; 2 EHRR 1, para 31, ECtHR.
11 See, for example, *B v France* (1992) A 232–C; 16 EHRR 1, para 48, ECtHR. See also *X, Y and Z v UK* (1997) 24 EHRR 143, ECtHR.

Precedent and the 'living instrument'

6.7   Convention law does not share the common law doctrine of *stare decisis*, which formally makes legal rulings binding as precedents.[12] As a matter of general practice, however, the ECtHR usually follows its own previous rulings, but where it considers that convincing reasons exist it can depart from an earlier judgment.[13] One of the principal reasons for the latter course is where the ECtHR considers that it is necessary to reflect changing social conditions. Thus, the ECtHR ensures that Convention law does not become sterile, by treating the Convention as a 'living instrument' and re-interpreting it as necessary in the light of present day conditions.[14]

Positive and negative obligations

6.8   The Convention is mainly concerned with restraining the state (negatively) from interference in the enjoyment of victims' rights. In some instances, however, these negative obligations are extended so as to create obligations to take some positive action in order to protect or facilitate the enjoyment of rights. Understanding this distinction, and the limited scope of positive obligations, is crucial to an appreciation of the effects of Convention rights.[15]

Source of positive obligations

6.9   Under the Convention, the concept of positive obligations arises generally from the requirement under article 1 for the state to 'secure' the rights and freedoms set out in the Convention. Although article 1 is not given direct effect in domestic law under the Human Rights Act 1998, there seems no reason to doubt that the obligation under HRA

---

12   Rulings of domestic courts under the Human Rights Act 1998, including those which apply Convention law, will be subject to *stare decisis*. But if Strasbourg case-law changes, domestic courts will be obliged to take this into account under HRA 1998 s2, so that the usual binding effect of *stare decisis* must be modified.

13   See generally *Cossey v UK* (1990) Series A No 184; 13 EHRR 622, para 35, ECtHR. See *Z v UK* [2001] 2 FCR 246, para 100, ECtHR, where the court appeared to accept that a previous ruling had been based on a misunderstanding of English law.

14   *Tyrer v UK* at note 10 above, para 31.

15   See para 2.12 onwards for positive obligations arising under article 8.

1998 s6 for public authorities to act[16] compatibly with the Convention rights will have similar effect. Moreover, positive obligations are inherent in the nature of some of the Convention rights. The drafting of a few articles makes this explicit.[17] In other cases, the obligation has arisen from interpretation through case-law, arising from the relative importance of certain Convention rights.[18] Article 8 derives the notion of a positive obligation from the concept of respect.[19] In principle, it would seem that positive obligations are capable of arising under article 1/1, as well as under article 14.[20] Article 6 inherently has positive elements to it, in the requirements for a fair trial.

Scope of positive obligations

6.10   The scope of positive obligations is not clear-cut, varying considerably from case to case. National authorities have a wide margin of appreciation in such matters.[21] It is therefore not possible to approach this in a generalistic way. Even where a positive obligation can be established, the extent of it will not be unlimited, and in a housing case it is likely to be fairly limited.[22]

Legal aid

6.11   One practical area in which a positive obligation may be important is in relation to legal assistance. There is no general right to legal aid under the Convention, but in certain circumstances it can be possible to establish a right to assistance. This may arise under article 6,[23] but it has also arisen under article 8.[24]

---

16 This term includes omissions: HRA 1998 s6(6).

17 See, for example, the protection by law of the right to life under article 2(1).

18 See, for example, *Z v UK* [2001] 2 FCR 246, ECtHR , in relation to the obligation under article 3 to intervene in order to protect children from abuse by their parents.

19 See para 2.12, above.

20 In relation to article 14, see the *Belgian Linguistic* case (1979–1980) Series A No 5; 1 EHRR 241, para I B 9, ECtHR.

21 *Abdulaziz, Cabales and Balkandali v UK* (1985) Series A No 94; 7 EHRR 471, para 67, ECtHR.

22 See, for example, *Marzari v Italy* (1999) 28 EHRR CD175, above at para 1.35.

23 See generally para 4.10 onwards, above.

24 *Airey v Ireland* (1979) Series A No 32; 2 EHRR 305, ECtHR.

Horizontal effect

6.12 A positive obligation may mean that the state becomes obliged to intervene in the relations between private persons, the so-called horizontal effect.[25]

Entrenched, absolute and qualified rights

6.13 In a formal sense, all the rights and freedoms guaranteed in the Convention have equal standing, but there are differences between them, as follows.

Entrenched rights

6.14 Under most of the Convention articles, states enjoy rights of exemption ('derogation') in times of public emergency.[26] A few of the Convention rights, however, are in general non-derogable, and thus entrenched,[27] but this does not apply to any of the Convention rights described at paras 1.15–1.18 above. Until recently, the UK had one derogation, though it was not relevant in a housing context.[28]

Absolute rights

6.15 Most of the Convention rights are subject to some qualification or limitation, and this is the case in relation to all the Convention rights described at paras 1.15–1.18 above. In contrast, a few of the other rights, or aspects of them, are absolute in nature.[29]

Qualified rights

6.16 All of the Convention rights described at paras 1.15–1.18 above are subject to some inherent qualification or limitation. In some cases, the

---

25 *X and Y v Netherlands* (1985) Series A No 91; 8 EHRR 235, ECtHR. See para 2.19 above.
26 Article 15(1).
27 See article 15(2). They include articles 2 and 3.
28 This related to article 5(3): see Human Rights Act 1998 Sch 3. The derogation was withdrawn on 26 February 2001, and the HRA 1998 consequently amended by SI 2001 No 1216.
29 See, for example, the prohibition of ill-treatment under article 3, and the right to hold beliefs under article 9.

express terms of the right provide for this.[30] In others, the limitation arises by implication.[31] The practical effect of this is that even if an interference with these rights can be established, the state may be able to justify the infringement. This gives rise to one of the essential features of the Convention – indeed, of any developed system of law – the balancing of interests and rights between different persons.[32]

6.17   The Convention also contains a number of general qualifying provisions, although these are unlikely to have any current bearing in housing cases. First, states are permitted to make reservations, to the extent to which any provision of domestic law does not conform with any provision of the Convention.[33] General reservations are not permitted. The UK presently has one reservation, though it is not relevant in a housing context.[34] Second, there is a specific power of restriction on the political activity of foreigners.[35] Third, there is a general provision which prevents persons from abusing any of the rights in order to destroy or damage the Convention rights.[36] Fourth, there is a prohibition against the use by the state of permissible restrictions on Convention rights for improper purposes.[37]

6.18   Where a Convention right is not subject to specific express limitations,[38] it may be subject to a limitation arising by implication. In a housing context, the most important example of this is article 6.[39]

Fair balance

6.19   The balancing of interests, and the search for a fair balance, is an inherent and important part of the Convention. Several articles (including articles 8 and 1/1) individually provide for balances to be struck in determining their operation; but the search for a fair balance, between the individual's rights and the broader interests of the community, has been said to be inherent in the Convention as a

---

30 See, for example, article 8(2).
31 See below.
32 See Fair balance at para 6.19 below.
33 Article 57.
34 This relates to article 2/1: Human Rights Act 1998 Sch 3.
35 Article 16.
36 Article 17 – which has hardly ever been used.
37 Article 18 – also rarely used, and difficult to prove.
38 Express limitations, for example, under article 8, are exhaustive: *Golder v UK* (1975) Series A No 18; 1 EHRR 524 para 44, ECtHR.
39 See para 4.13, above.

whole.[40] In practice, this balance gives the state considerable latitude to interfere in the enjoyment of an individual's rights, particularly because the state[41] is often accorded a wide area of discretion in determining how the balance should be struck.[42]

Margin of appreciation

6.20   The Convention concept of a margin of appreciation simply means the area of discretion which the Strasbourg authorities allow each state in determining how to secure observance within their jurisdictions of the various Convention rights and freedoms. This is a mark of subsidiarity, namely that the Strasbourg authorities leave it to each state in the first instance to determine what is required.[43] The Strasbourg authorities will only intervene when, on a supervisory review, they determine that the state has gone beyond acceptable bounds.

Application under Human Rights Act 1998

6.21   The margin of appreciation does not in itself apply to the task of our domestic courts under the Human Rights Act 1998.[44] This is because the rationale for the margin of appreciation is that national authorities are better placed than the Strasbourg authorities to know about and determine local conditions. It is clear, however, that domestic courts are applying an analogous principle, long recognised in public law, whereby they recognise and respect an area of discretion in which public authorities are allowed to act without intervention from the courts.[45] Accordingly, the application of the margin of appreciation by the Strasbourg authorities is relevant, by analogy, to the use of the Convention rights under the Human Rights Act 1998.

Varying extent of margin

6.22   The extent of the margin varies. The narrower the margin, the sharper the level of scrutiny adopted by the ECtHR. The broader the

---

40 *Sporrong and Lönnroth v Sweden* (1982) Series A No 52, para 69, ECtHR.

41 Especially elected bodies, such as parliament, the executive and local government.

42 See margin of appreciation, and proportionality, below.

43 See, for example, *Handyside v UK* (1976) Series A No 24; 1 EHRR 737, para 48, ECtHR.

44 *R v A (No 2)* [2001] UKHL 25; [2001] 2 WLR 1546, para 58 (Lord Hope), HL.

45 See, for example, *Poplar Housing and Regeneration Community Association Ltd* v *Donoghue* [2001] EWCA Civ 595; [2001] 3 WLR 183, CA.

margin, the less intense the scrutiny. The breadth of the margin depends upon the circumstances. Factors which affect the breadth of the margin include the relative importance of the right within the Convention, the effect on the individual, the extent of any consensus between the contracting states, and the suitability of the issue for judicial determination. Under article 8, there is a wide margin as to the requirements for effective 'respect',[46] but a narrow margin when it comes to intimate aspects of private life.[47] Under article 1/1, national authorities enjoy a wide margin in the implementation of social and economic policies in the context of leasehold reform.[48] Article 6(1) permits a certain margin in relation to the right of access to a court, provided this does not impair the very essence of the right.[49] Under article 14, some margin has been held to apply in assessing whether and to what extent differences in otherwise similar situations justify a different treatment in law.[50]

Proportionality

6.23   As a companion to the margin of appreciation, the principle of proportionality provides a means whereby the Strasbourg authorities limit and test the extent and exercise of the discretion given to national authorities in the justification of an interference with a Convention right. In short, the principle involves determining whether the relevant act or measure employed by the state is proportionate to the aim which the state is trying to achieve.[51] Put another way, this test requires an assessment whether the reasons given for the interference are both relevant and sufficient to justify it.[52] The principle applies under the Human Rights Act 1998.

Examples under article 8

6.24   Under article 8,[53] the refusal to grant a residence licence for occupation of a home was held to have been disproportionate because

46   *Abdulaziz, Cabales and Balkandali v UK* (1985) Series A No 94; 7 EHRR 471, ECtHR.
47   *Dudgeon v UK* (1981) Series A No 45; 4 EHRR 149, ECtHR.
48   *James v UK* (1986) Series A No 98; 8 EHRR 123, ECtHR.
49   *Osman v UK* (2000) 29 EHRR 245, para 147, ECtHR.
50   *Rasmussen v Denmark* (1984) Series A No 87; 7 EHRR 371, ECtHR.
51   See, for example, *Handyside v UK* (1976) Series A No 24; 1 EHRR 737, paras 48–49 and 97, ECtHR.
52   See, for example, *Chapman v UK* (2001) 10 BHRC 48, para 90, ECtHR.
53   See generally para 2.48 onwards above.

insufficient weight was given to the applicants' personal circumstances.[54] Entry by police into a person's home was held to have been disproportionate because the police failed to check whether the information they had been given was correct, and because they should have become aware that there was no need for their presence.[55]

Examples under article 1/1

6.25 In several cases under article 1/1, the ECtHR has considered the balance of interests which accompanies the test of proportionality.[56] In *Sporrong and Lönnroth v Sweden*,[57] the test was expressed by the notion of the 'fair balance' that must be struck between the demands of the general interest of the community and the requirements of the protection of the individual's fundamental rights. The requisite balance is not found if the person concerned has had to bear 'an individual and excessive burden'. In *James v UK*,[58] the court reiterated this need for a fair balance, and held that a measure must be both appropriate for achieving its aim, and not disproportionate to it.

Other examples

6.26 Proportionality has also arisen in the context of article 6, controlling the provision of immunity from legal claims,[59] and in relation to limitation periods.[60] There have also been several examples of cases under article 14.[61]

Waiver of Convention rights

6.27 It is possible for most Convention rights to be waived, but arguments to this effect are subjected to the most detailed scrutiny. Even where

54 *Gillow v UK* (1986) Series A No 109; 11 EHRR 335, ECtHR.
55 *McLeod v UK* (1999) 27 EHRR 493, ECtHR.
56 See generally para 3.12 onwards, above.
57 (1982) Series A No 52; 5 EHRR 35, ECtHR.
58 (1986) Series A No 98; 8 EHRR 123, ECtHR.
59 *Fayed v UK* (1994) Series A 294–B; 18 EHRR 393. See also *Osman v UK* (1999) 1 LGLR 431, ECtHR, where a Court of Appeal ruling was held to have been disproportionate; but see now *Z v UK* [2001] 2 FCR 246, ECtHR.
60 *Stubbings v UK* (1997) 23 EHRR 213, ECtHR.
61 See, for example, *Rasmussen v Denmark* (1984) Series A No 87; 7 EHRR 371, ECtHR. *Abdulaziz, Cabales and Balkandali v UK* (1985) Series A No 94; 7 EHRR 471, ECtHR. *Gaygusuz v Austria* (1997) 23 EHRR 364, ECtHR.

the nature of a Convention rights permits waiver, it may be prevented if it would run counter to the public interest.[62]

6.28   A waiver may be express, or implied.[63] The latter, however, is regarded particularly critically. In one case, for example,[64] an application for state compensation in respect of an accident at work was held not to imply that the applicant had waived her rights under article 8 with regard to her medical records. A succession of cases has laid down the requirement that any waiver has to be established in 'an unequivocal manner'.[65]

6.29   In *Deweer v Belgium*,[66] the court held that while the right of access to a tribunal under article 6 was capable of being waived, one of the conditions for an effective waiver was an absence of pressure.[67] The effective waiver of a procedural right also requires 'minimum guarantees commensurate to its importance'.[68]

Remedies: 'just satisfaction'

6.30   Where a violation has been found, and domestic law does not allow full reparation to be made, article 41 requires the court, where necessary, to afford 'just satisfaction' to the injured party. This power extends only to an award of pecuniary compensation. The principles upon which the court does this under article 41 are directly applicable to awards of damages by national courts under the Human Rights Act 1998.[69]

Cases where no damages are awarded

6.31   In many instances, the mere finding of a violation has been held to be a sufficient remedy in itself. This is so particularly if the violation is

---

62   *Håkansson and Sturesson v Sweden* (1990) Series A No 171; 13 EHRR 1, paras 66–67, ECtHR. *Schuler-Sgraggen v Switzerland* (1993) Series A No 263; 16 EHRR 405, para 58, ECtHR.

63   Also known as tacit waivers.

64   *MS v Sweden* (1999) 28 EHRR 313, ECtHR.

65   See, for example, *Oberschlick v Austria* (1991) Series A No 204; 19 EHRR 389, para 51, ECtHR.

66   (1980) Series A No 35; 2 EHRR 439, para 49, ECtHR.

67   See also *Le Compte, Van Leuven and De Meyere v Belgium* (1981) Series A No 43; 4 EHRR 1, para 59, ECtHR.

68   *Pfeiffer and Plankl v Austria* (1992) Series A No 227; 14 EHRR 692, para 37, ECtHR.

69   See s8(4). See also para 14.53 onwards, below.

technical rather than substantial, and where the applicant has suffered no worse than a feeling of injustice.[70]

Court's discretion

6.32 The ECtHR's discretion is exercised in a broad way, according to the circumstances in each case. Damages are often said to be assessed on an equitable basis. Detailed principles are hard to come by. Relevant factors include the nature and actual effect of the violation,[71] and the conduct of the applicant.[72] Awards of damages in national law are relevant but not decisive.[73]

Assessment of damages

6.33 Damages are awarded under two heads: pecuniary and non-pecuniary loss. Pecuniary loss includes loss of income, past and future,[74] diminution in the value of property,[75] and future medical costs.[76] Non-pecuniary loss (also referred to as moral damage) includes pain and suffering, distress, anxiety, feelings of injustice and frustration, and damage to way of life. Aggravated or exemplary damages have not been awarded. Awards for non-pecuniary loss have not generally been large, though in *Z v UK*[77] the ECtHR awarded £32,000 to each of four children who had suffered very serious abuse and neglect over a four year period. In *Halford v UK*,[78] the applicant was awarded £10,000 for intrusion into privacy caused by the tapping of telephone calls at work.

---

70 See, for example, *Robins v UK* (1998) 26 EHRR 527, ECtHR.
71 See, for example, *Scott v Spain* (1997) 24 EHRR 391, ECtHR.
72 *A v Denmark* (1996) 22 EHRR 458, ECtHR.
73 *Z v UK* [2001] 2 FCR 246, para 120, ECtHR.
74 *Young, James and Webster v UK* (1982) Series A No 55; 5 EHRR 201, ECtHR. *Open Door Counselling Ltd and Dublin Well Woman Clinic Ltd v Ireland* (1992) Series A No 246; 15 EHRR 244, ECtHR.
75 *Sporrong and Lönnroth v Sweden* (1984) Series A No 88; 7 EHRR 256, ECtHR. *Pine Valley Developments Ltd v Ireland* (1991) Series A No 222; 14 EHRR 319, ECtHR. *Hentrich v France* (1996) Series A No 322; 21 EHRR 199, ECtHR.
76 *Z v UK* [2001] 2 FCR 246, ECtHR.
77 See note 76 above.
78 (1997) 24 EHRR 523, ECtHR.

Causation

6.34   Causation must be established between the violation and the loss.[79] This may be difficult to achieve where the assessment would depend upon speculation as to how events may have unfolded if the violation had not occurred,[80] but an award may still be made even if there is a large number of imponderables.[81] Quantification may also be a problem, but the ECtHR has developed a broad concept of loss of opportunities which is used where the assessment is difficult.[82]

---

79 See, for example, *Kampanis v Greece* (1995) Series A No 325; 21 EHRR 43, ECtHR.
80 See, for example, *Saunders v UK* (1997) 23 EHRR 313, ECtHR.
81 *Z v UK* at note 76 above.
82 *Sporrong and Lönnroth v Sweden* at note 75 above.

PART II

Practical issues for human rights in housing

Access to and allocation of housing

Introduction

7.1   Provision and allocation of housing are still important functions carried out by local authorities. For those who are homeless, provision is made for assistance under the Housing Act 1996 Part VII. Longer-term housing needs may be met through allocation to local authority housing or that belonging to registered social landlords (RSLs). About 16% of the current housing stock in England and Wales is owned by local authorities and 5% by RSLs. Some statutory controls over allocations are provided for in the Housing Act 1996 Part VI.

7.2   In making decisions as to who will be housed and where, both local authorities and registered social landlords exercise much discretion. This chapter will examine how, if at all, the exercise of that discretion may be challenged under the Convention. In addition two further pieces of legislation which provide in some circumstances for access to housing are considered: the Children Act 1989 and the Asylum and Immigration Act 1999.

Homelessness

7.3   Primary provision for the homeless in England and Wales is made through the Housing Act (HA) 1996 Part VII. This requires local housing authorities to provide accommodation for those who fall within the definition of homelessness and are otherwise eligible in terms of their immigration status, fall within the priority need categories and are not intentionally homeless.[1] The primary duty under HA 1996 Part VII to those who satisfy these tests is to provide accommodation for a maximum of 2 years.

7.4   As has already been discussed, article 8 has been interpreted as falling short of recognising a right *to* a home.[2] The provisions of the Housing Act 1996, accordingly provide a structure of protection for the homeless which undoubtedly goes further than is required under the Convention, and also provides greater substantive rights than in many other European states.[3]

7.5   The limitations on the interpretation of article 8 accordingly make

---

1   See generally, *Homelessness and Allocations,* Arden and Hunter (LAG 5th edition, 1997 (6th edition forthcoming in 2002)).

2   See paras 2.5–2.10, above and *X v Federal Republic of Germany* (1956) 1 YB 202, EComHR. Compare *Mazarri v Italy* (1999) 28 EHRR CD 175, discussed below at para. 7.20.

3   Compare French right to a home – the '*Loi Besson*'.

it difficult to mount challenges to decisions made by authorities under HA 1996 Part VII. Thus findings that an applicant is, for example, not in priority need or is intentionally homeless, and therefore excluded from substantive assistance under HA 1996 Part VII do not of themselves leave any room for challenge for breach of the Convention, since article 8 has not been engaged at this point. In *Ekinci v Hackney LBC*[3a] Pill LJ said at para 16:

> There is no breach of article 8(1) in Parliament enacting a scheme of priorities whereby applications for accommodation by homeless persons are to be determined by local housing authorities whose resources will inevitably be limited. In assessing priorities, Parliament is entitled to take into account considerations, such as vulnerability, which may or may not have an impact on family life, as well as those which inevitably do.

Internal reviews and appeals

7.6   One area which might have seemed ripe to challenge is the fact that challenges to homelessness decisions are made through an internal review procedure, thus potentially engaging article 6. However, before article 6 can be engaged the applicant must establish that a civil right, for instance, one arising in private law, has been interfered with.[4] The rights of the homeless are unlikely to be considered as falling within this ambit, and are more likely to be considered 'public' in nature.[5]

7.7   Furthermore, even if the rights are considered private rights, and thus falling within the ambit of article 6, challenges to homelessness decisions, although requiring first an internal review, may then be appealed to the county court. It is likely in the light of the decision in *R (on the application of Johns and McLellan) v Bracknell Forrest DC*[6] in relation to the internal review for introductory tenancies,[7] that the internal review followed by the right to appeal to the county court on a point of law (essentially the same basis as for judicial review[8]) would satisfy the requirements of article 6.

3a   [2001] EWCA Civ 776, CA, rejecting a claim under s189(1)(b) of the 1996 Act that an applicant was in priority need because his 17-year-old wife was a dependent child.

4   See para 4.3, above.

5   See paras 4.4 and 4.5, above.

6   (2001) 33 HLR 45, QBD (currently pending appeal). See also *R (on the application of Holding and Barnes plc) v Secretary of State for the Environment, Transport and the Regions* [2001] UKHL 23, (2001) *Times* 10 May.

7   See para 9.19, below.

8   See *Begum v Tower Hamlets* (1999) 32 HLR 445, CA.

7.8   One issue that could be considered is whether the 21-day time limit imposed by HA 1996 s204(2) gives applicants a sufficient opportunity to exercise their rights to appeal. The time limit is very tight and may make it very difficult for legal aid to be obtained within this time frame. This has been acknowledged as short, indeed 'draconian, as some might think'.[9] Unless the statute in question gives a court power to extend time (which HA 1996 s204 does not), the court's usual power to extend time under Civil Procedure Rules (CPR) 3.1 does not apply to a statutory time limits.[10] Accordingly, the time limit must be strictly complied with.

7.9   In *Airey v Ireland*[11] the ECtHR said at paragraph 24 of the judgment:

> the convention is intended to guarantee not rights that are theoretical or illusory but rights that are practical and effective ...This is particularly so of the right of access to the courts ...

In that case the applicant was not entitled to legal aid to obtain a separation from her husband in the High Court.[12] It could be argued, particularly if the evidence showed that the time limit was having a detrimental effect on the ability of applicants to obtain legal assistance in filing appeals under HA 1996 s204, that the time limit made the right to appeal theoretical or illusory.

7.10   It has recently been held that an applicant who wants to challenge the suitability of an offer of accommodation under HA 1996 s202(1)(f) must first decline the offer. He or she could not move into the property offered and then pursue his or her rights to internal review and then appeal to the county court.[13] The decision was made on the basis of an interpretation of HA 1996 s193, which sets out the circumstances in which an authority's duty towards an applicant is discharged. Is the requirement to take such a risk, ie, rejecting the offer of accommodation, before pursuing rights to appeal, not a disproportionate disincentive to pursuing such rights? Furthermore, at this stage in the process of deciding a homelessness application, when a definite offer of accommodation has been made, it is at least arguable that a private right has accrued, thus engaging article 6.[14]

---

9 Per Tucker J, *R v Brent LBC ex p O'Connor* (1998) 31 HLR 923, QBD at p925.
10 *Honig v Lewisham LBC* (1958) 122 JPJ 302 and *Gwynedd CC v Grunshaw* (1999) 32 HLR 610, CA. See also *O'Connor* at note 9 above.
11 (1979) Series A No 32.
12 See also *Bates v Croydon LBC* [2001] EWCA Civ 134; (2001) 33 HLR forthcoming, discussed at para. 9.11, below.
13 *Alghile v Westminster CC* (2001) *Times* 9 March, CA.
14 Compare, however, *Mohram Ali v Tower Hamlets LBC* [1993] QB 407; 24 HLR

7.11   The position of homeless families being evicted from temporary accommodation prior to any internal review or county court appeal being heard may also be considered. While the 1996 Act provides that an authority may continue to house pending internal review and appeal[15], does the termination of such right when the authority refuses to exercise their discretion and pursue possession (ie, terminate the private law right to continue to occupy the temporary accommodation) effectively make the right to internal review and appeal illusory?

Respect for family life

7.12   It has always been the case that the homeless persons provisions have been about keeping families together[16], and in that way respecting family life. However, where family relationships have broken down issues may arise over priority need which have an impact on family life.

7.13   Under HA 1996 s189(1)(b) an applicant has priority need where he or she is 'a person with whom dependent children reside or might reasonably be expected to reside'. Where parents have separated the question arises as to whether they are dependent children who do reside or can reasonably be expected to reside with each parent, or with only one. In *W v UK*[17] the ECtHR stated that 'the mutual enjoyment by parent and child of each other's company constitutes a fundamental element of family life'.

7.14   In interpreting the priority need provisions of HA 1996 s189, in *Bishop*,[18] where the parents had agreed that the children should split their time between each of them, the authority decided that the children were not dependent on the father. In reaching this decision they took into account that the children were adequately housed with the mother, that she received income support and child benefit for them, and that the applicant, who was unemployed, did not have

474, CA; *Tower Hamlets LBC v Abdi* (1992) 25 HLR 461, CA; and *Hackney LBC v Lambourne* (1992) 25 HLR 172, CA; where the decision whether accommodation offered was suitable was said to be part of the public law decision making of an authority.

15 See Housing Act 1996 ss188(3) and 204(4). The courts have been very reluctant to interfere with the exercise of this discretion, which is rarely exercised in favour of an applicant: *R v Camden LBC ex p Mohammed* (1997) 30 HLR 315, QBD; *R v Hammersmith & Fulham LBC ex p Fleck* (1997) 30 HLR 679, QBD; *R v Brighton and Hove BC ex p Nacion* (1999) 31 HLR 315, QBD.

16 *R v Hillingdon LBC ex p Islam* [1983] 1 AC 688, HL; *R v Ealing LBC ex p Surdonja* (1998) 31 HLR 686, QBD.

17 (1987) 10 EHRR 29, at para. 59.

18 *R v Westminster CC ex p Bishop* (1996) 29 HLR 546, QBD.

financial means of supporting them. The court upheld all these matters as being relevant to the decision.

7.15   Even where joint residence has been ordered[19] this does not necessarily mean that the children can reasonably be expected to reside with both parents. In *Doyle*,[20] following a relationship breakdown, a joint residence order had been made by the court under which the four children of the parents were to spend half the week with each parent. The father was homeless. The decision of the authority that the children could not reasonably be expected to reside with the father was upheld by the court. The authority had applied the correct test and taken into account the residence order. In reaching the decision that the children could not be expected to reside with him, the authority were entitled to take into account the shortage of housing stock in their area and to conclude that under-occupation even for part of the week could only be permitted if fully justified.

7.16   In these circumstances could it be argued that the authority, in refusing to accept an applicant as being in priority need was denying the right to family life? Such an interpretation would effectively require a positive obligation on the state, for instance, to provide a home in this situation, which may go further than is presently required by the Convention. However, positive obligations have been imposed in relation to the right to family life. In *Ahmut v Netherlands*[21] the Dutch authorities refused to grant a residence permit to a Dutch national's son. The son was a Moroccan national. The ECtHR stated at paragraph 63 of the judgment that there:

> may be positive obligations inherent in effective 'respect' for family life. However, the boundaries between the State's positive and negative obligations under this provision do not lend themselves to precise definition... In both contexts regard must be had to the fair balance that has to be struck between the competing interests of the individual and the community as a whole; and in both contexts the State enjoys a certain margin of appreciation.

7.17   Given this wide margin, the decisions in *Bishop* and *Doyle* are likely to fall within the margin.[22]

---

19   Under the Children Act 1989 s8.
20   *R v Oxford CC ex p Doyle* (1997) 30 HLR 506, QBD.
21   (1997) 24 EHRR 62.
22   See also the decision in *R v Swale BC ex p Marchant* (1998) 32 HLR 26, QBD; 32 HLR 856, CA, where a claim for housing benefit based on the residence for part of the week was rejected. At first instance the judge rejected an argument that article 8 required the state to provide two homes both large enough to accommodate the children of parents who had separated.

Allocation of social housing

7.18   While Part VII of the Housing Act 1996 applies only to local housing authorities, access to long-term housing requires consideration not only of the decisions of local authorities but also of registered social landlords (RSLs). As stock transfer from local authorities increases (as is currently projected) RSLs will become an increasingly important sector of the housing market.

7.19   Where decisions regarding RSLs are concerned the most important preliminary issue will be whether they are considered to be public bodies falling within HRA 1998 s6. This is discussed further below in Chapter 13.

7.20   Beyond this, can any allocation decisions by local housing authorities or RSLs be said to be subject to the provisions of the Convention? Again the lack of any positive housing duty under article 8 will limit any basis for challenge. In *Marzari v Italy*[23] it could be argued that the court did recognise a positive obligation to provide housing, at least in the circumstances of someone who was severely disabled.[24] Even in those circumstances the obligation did not give rise to the right to be allocated any particular property. The court held it was not for them to interfere with decisions on the suitability of accommodation and 'no positive obligation for the local authorities can be inferred from article 8 to provide the applicant with a specific apartment'.

Exclusion lists

7.21   One particular allocation issue which has reportedly been concerning the Department of the Environment, Transport and the Regions (now the Department of Transport, Local Government and the Regions) as to its compatibility with the Convention, is the use of exclusion policies by local housing authorities. These may be used to prevent certain types of applicant, for example, those owing arrears of rent to the authority, or those with a history of anti-social behaviour, from accessing housing. The Housing Act 1996 s161(3) permits local housing authorities to decide 'what classes of persons are, or are not, qualifying persons' for the purposes of HA 1996 Part VI and accordingly qualified to be allocated accommodation by local authorities.

7.22   Some applicants who are found to fall within a particular class may effectively be denied access to local authority accommodation

23   (1999) 28 EHRR CD 175, EComHR.
24   See para 2.16, above.

in the area in which they live, however great their housing need. Furthermore, as information has been increasingly shared between social landlords, this could in practice mean that some applicants might be excluded by other RSLs and local authorities in the particular area.

7.23   It is not clear whether such blanket bans could be challengeable under the Convention. Given article 8 requires 'respect for the home' it is arguable that simply denying access to a waiting list under which a different home might be allocated does not amount to a breach. Nonetheless the government sought to change the law in the Homes Bill 2001, so that all persons who satisfy the immigration law tests would be eligible to go on a housing waiting list, although certain groups including those evicted for rent arrears or anti-social behaviour would have a reduced priority on the list.[25]

Children Act 1989

7.24   The Children Act (CA) 1989 is not primarily a housing measure, being concerned much more with the rights and needs of children.[26] It may, however, come into play where families are homeless and unable to obtain assistance under HA 1996 Part VII, because the parents have, for example, been found intentionally homeless. It also imposes duties on local authorities where under 18-year-olds are homeless and estranged from their parents and for children leaving care.[27]

7.25   The duties under CA 1989 ss17 and 20 will arise because a child is in need. Under the principles of CA 1989 the needs of the child will be paramount.[28] It should be noted, however, that CA 1996 s17 only provides a 'target duty', with a power to house the parent of the child,[28a] while CA 1996 s20 provides a duty to provide accommodation for the child in need and not for the parents of the child.[28b] Accordingly it will not override the provisions of the Housing Act

25   The Homes Bill did not complete its stages through Parliament before the election of June 2001. See now the Homelessness Bill 2001, reintroduced in the subsequent Parliament.

26   For a detailed discussion of the implications of the Convention on family and child law, see *European Human Rights Law*, Starmer, chapters 19 and 20 (LAG, 1999); *Human Rights Act 1998: A practitioner's guide*, Baker, ed, *Family and Child Law*, Henderson (Sweet and Maxwell, 1998).

27   See principally CA 1989 ss17 and 20.

28   CA 1989 s1.

28a *R (on the application of A) v Lambeth LBC* (2001) 33 HLR 60, QBD.

28b *R (on the application of G) v Barnet LBC* (2001) 33 HLR 59, CA.

1996 relating to the allocation of housing. The authority must take reasonable steps to enable the child to live with his or her family, or to have contact with them.[29] But such a service must be appropriate to the child's needs, rather than the family's needs.

7.26   In considering what support to provide for children in need, local authorities are required to consider the needs of the individual child over and above the needs of the family: *R v Tower Hamlets LBC ex p Bradford*.[30] So, for example, while the parents may wish to live in a particular area, a child may need to move. This could possibly give rise to an argument of breach of article 8.

7.27   There is no requirement in the Children Act 1989 for consultation with parents prior to deciding to provide accommodation under CA 1989 s20. Again, this situation could give rise to claims of violation of article 8.[31] It should be noted, however, that generally in relation to decisions on what is in the best interests of children the European Court of Human Rights has allowed states a wide margin of appreciation.[32] It is not clear to what extent pressure on the financial resources of a local authority (see, for example, *R v Gloucestershire County Council ex p Barry*[33]) would be considered sufficient justification under article 8(2) for what may be a violation of the right to family life.

Asylum-seekers

7.28   Since 4 April 2000, asylum-seekers have fallen entirely outside the ambit of the Housing Act 1996 and the Children Act 1989. Provision for their housing is made through the Asylum and Immigration Act 1999. Prior to that certain 'at-port' asylum-seekers were permitted to apply for assistance as homeless under HA 1996 Part VII. The courts in a long battle with the government[34] sought to limit the impact of the withdrawal of benefits to 'in-country' asylum-seekers (who are

29   CA 1989 Sch 2, para 10.

30   (1997) 29 HLR 756.

31   See also *R v Kingston-upon-Thames RBLC ex p T* [1994] 1 FLR 798, *Olsson v Sweden* (1988) 11 EHRR 259, ECtHR.

32   See, for example, *Reime v Sweden* (1992)16 EHRR 155, ECtHR. Compare with *Berrehab v The Netherlands* (1989) 11 EHRR 322, ECtHR.

33   [1997] 2 WLR 459; (1997) 1 CCLR 7, QBD.

34   See *R v Hammersmith and Fulham LBC ex p M* (1997) 30 HLR 10, CA; and *R v Secretary of State for Social Security ex p B* (1996) 29 HLR 129, CA; and *R v Kensington and Chelsea LBC ex p Kihara* (1996) 29 HLR 147, CA.

also not allowed to work), and felt able to do this without 'resort to the European Convention of Human Rights' since the regulations withdrawing benefits to asylum-seekers rendered asylum rights nugatory or contemplated 'for some a life so destitute that to my mind no civilised nation can tolerate it': per Neill LJ in *ex p B*. Accordingly provision was made for in-country asylum-seekers under either the Children Act 1989 or the National Assistance Act 1948.[35]

7.29   The piecemeal system of support developed through the courts was replaced by the Asylum and Immigration Act (AIA) 1999, which provides for all asylum-seekers if otherwise destitute to be provided with support and accommodation. Accommodation is provided through arrangements with local authorities or other providers, such as registered social landlords or private landlords. Asylum-seekers also receive support to pay for their living costs, mostly in the form of vouchers.

7.30   The provision of accommodation and vouchers, providing for a very basic standard of living, coupled with the fact that there is no right to housing under article 8 makes it unlikely that a challenge to the legality of AIA 1999 based on the Convention is likely to be successful. However there have been reports of some asylum-seekers being offered and moving in to properties of an appalling standard. Any enforcement of private law rights to repair[36] will be almost impossible for asylum-seekers, given their lack of security of tenure and difficulties of access to the legal system. Could this be considered a lack of respect for the home?

7.31   Furthermore the policy of the government has been to disperse asylum-seekers throughout the country. This may on occasion lead to at least extended families being split, and asylum-seekers being unable to access the support of friends and community groups. Could this be considered a breach of respect for family and private life?[37]

---

35   *R v Hammersmith and Fulham LBC ex p M* (1997) 30 HLR 10, CA.
36   See chapter 10, below.
37   See, for example, *Beldjoudi v France* (1992) Series A No 234–A, although in that case the applicant was being deported from a country where all his family lived, to a country where he did not speak the language.

CHAPTER 8

Security of tenure and possession

Introduction

8.1   This chapter will consider a whole range of issues which arise around security of tenure and the recovery of possession. These will be examined for each of the different tenure groups (private sector tenants, social sector tenants, owner occupiers and trespassers) together with the particular problems of travellers. In addition, issues around succession to tenancies will be considered.

8.2   An eviction of a person from their home will ordinarily be an interference with the right under article 8,[1] furthermore where that person has property rights in relation to the home (for instance, is a tenant, leaseholder or freeholder) there will also be an interference under article 1/1. This is not to say that eviction is prohibited by the Convention, since it may be justified. On the other hand where the landlord of the property is a private person and security of tenure provisions restrict his or her rights to possession he or she may also be able to claim interference with the rights under article 1/1 because of the limitation of the right to gain possession. Again such limitations of property rights may be justified.

8.3   Rights to security of tenure differ, primarily in accordance with the identity of the landlord and the date the tenant moved into the property.[2] For private sector tenants the effects of the Housing Acts 1988 and 1996 has been to limit severely the security of tenure that tenants have, compared with that under the Rent Act 1977. Within each of the relevant Acts which grants security of tenure there are also exemptions which mean that some occupiers, for example, in the private sector those with resident landlords, do not have security, and can be evicted at will by the landlord.

8.4   In *Larkos v Cyprus*[3] the ECtHR considered whether differences between different categories of occupiers could be justified. The applicant, a retired civil servant had been the tenant of the Cypriot government for some 30 years. The tenancy was in fairly standard terms, but provided that the tenancy could be terminated should that

---

1   See further the discussion at para 2.36 and see *R (on the application of John and Mclellan) v Bracknell Forrest DC* (2001) 33 HLR 45, at para 39 and *Lambeth LBC v Howard* (2001) 33 HLR 58, CA at para 32. Note the discussion below, para 8.18 as to the applicability to private landlords.

2   See the Housing Act 1985 for tenants of local authorities, the Housing Acts 1985 and 1988 for tenants of registered social landlords and the Rent Act 1977 and the Housing Act 1988 (as amended by the Housing Act 1996) for the tenants of private landlords.

3   (1999) 7 BHRC 244, ECtHR.

applicant be transferred to a district other than the one in which the property was situated.

8.5 When following his retirement, the government sought possession of the house, the applicant claimed that he was a statutory tenant under the Rent Control Law 1983. In court the government argued that the law did not apply as the house had been allocated to him by administrative order because of his position in the civil service. The court upheld this argument. Interpretation of the law led it to conclude that it only bound private owners of property and not the government. An appeal to the Supreme Court of Cyprus was dismissed.

8.6 The ECtHR found that there had been a breach of article 14 in conjunction with article 8, in that as a government tenant the applicant had been unlawfully discriminated against in the enjoyment of his right to respect for his home.[4] In considering whether the difference in treatment could be justified the court first looked closely at the terms of the tenancy:

> the lease makes no reference to the fact that the property was let to [the applicant] in his capacity of civil servant or that the subsistence of the lease was dependent on his continued employment in the civil service … [The transfer clause] was introduced to protect his own rather than the government's interests. Moreover, the lease is silent on the consequences resulting for the applicant's retirement or resignation from the civil service. Nor would it appear that the rent to be paid by the applicant was fixed at a preferential rate on account of his status … Having regard to these considerations and in particular to the fact that the terms of the lease indicate clearly that the government rented the property in a private law capacity, the court considers that Mr Larkos can claim with justification to be in a relevantly similar situation to that of other private tenants who rent accommodation from private landlords.

8.7 The court dismissed the attempts by the Cyprus government to justify the difference in treatment:

> While the court accepts that a measure which has the effect of treating differently persons in a relevantly similar situation may be justified on public interest ground, it considers that in the instant case the respondent government have not provided any convincing explanation of how the general interest will be served by evicting the applicant. They have not pointed to any preponderant interest which would warrant the withdrawal from the applicant of the protection accorded to other tenants …

---

4   The court did not find it necessary to consider whether, additionally, there had been a breach of article 14 in conjunction with article 1/1.

Arguments that tenancies of state-owned properties were different because they were not motivated by profit were dismissed, since there was no evidence that this tenancy was not let at market rate and as a private law transaction.

> The court would also note that the legislation was intended as a measure of social protection for tenants ... A decision not to extend that protection to government tenants living side by side with tenants in privately-owned dwellings requires specific justification ... However, the government have not adduced any reasonable and objective justification for the distinction which meets the requirements of article14 of the Convention, even having regard to their margin of appreciation in the area of the control of property.

8.8   Returning to housing law status within this country, the *Larkos* case raises the questions: first, whether the differences between different forms of tenure can be justified; and second, whether specific exemptions within statutes are justified. It seems likely that the main differences, for instance, lesser security for private sector tenants are justifiable, given the long-term aim of encouraging private landlords in to the market.[5] Some of the exemptions within Acts may also be clearly justifiable, for example, holiday lettings, student lettings and so on. The justification for excluding those with no cooking facilities (because there is no letting as a separate dwelling[6]) has recently been called in to question: see the dissenting judgment of Mance LJ in *Uratemp Ventures Ltd v Collins*.[7] Both the Rent Act 1977 and the Housing Act 1988 exclude Crown tenants from protection.[8] While there may be some circumstances why Crown tenants should be excluded, in others their position may be more analogous to those in *Larkos*.

Court procedures

8.9   Article 6 will always be relevant where possession is being sought, since what will be determined is a person's civil rights. Accordingly all possession hearings will require compliance with article 6(1).

---

5   Consider too, the accepted justification of the need for introductory tenancies to deal with anti-social behaviour: see para 9.22, below.
6   See the Housing Act 1988 s1, the Rent Act 1977 s1 and the Housing Act 1985 s79.
7   (2001) 33 HLR 4 at paras 61 and 62 (currently pending judgement on appeal).
8   Housing Act 1988 Sch 1 para 11; Rent Act 1977 s13.

8.10   One change that has had to be made in order to make procedures compliant with the Convention is to the accelerated possession procedure.[9] The accelerated possession procedure still remains for assured shorthold tenancies[10] allowing for possession without a court hearing. This, according to Treasury counsel, is compliant with article 6,[11] since possession can only be ordered without a hearing where the tenant admits there is no defence. In such a case there are no civil rights to be determined. If the tenant claims a defence then there is an entitlement to a public hearing.

8.11   The procedures have, however, been amended to allow for a hearing where the tenant seeks postponement of the date for possession beyond the minimum 14 day period, on the ground of exceptional hardship.[12] Such a hearing must be held before the date on which possession is to be given up.

8.12   Another area that has come under scrutiny, is the hearing of possession cases in chambers. The issue was raised in the case of *R (on the application of Pelling) v Bow County Court*,[13] where the applicant challenged both rule 39.2(3)(c) of the Civil Procedure Rules, which provides that:

> (3) A hearing, or any part of it, may be in private if – ...
>   (c) it involves confidential information (including information relating to personal financial matters) and publicity would damage that confidentiality ...

and the practice direction made in accordance with the rule that permits a claim by a landlord against one or more tenants or former tenants for the repossession of a dwelling house based on the non-payment of rent to be heard in private. The challenge was rejected since article 6 does not create absolute rights and this was an area in which there was some discretion for the national government.

8.13   Another procedural aspect of cases arises where defences to possession actions are struck out. In *Arogundade v Brent LBC*,[14] the tenant's reply and defence to a claim for possession (essentially

---

9   CCR, Ord 49, rr 6 and 6A were amended by the Civil Procedure (Amendment No 4) Rules 2000 SI No 2092. The amended procedure will be incorporated in to the new CPR 55, to be implemented on 15 October 2001.

10 But not since amendment to any grounds under the Housing Act 1988 Sch 2.

11 See *Journal of Housing Law, Possession proceedings and human rights – part 2*, Madge, p21 at p23 (Sweet and Maxwell, 2001).

12 Discretion is given to judges under the Housing Act 1980 s89.

13 [2001] UKHRR 165, QBD (Adminstrative Court).

14 March 2001 *Legal Action* 29.

arising out of a separate claim for damages for disrepair) was struck out for failing to disclose any reasonable basis for defending the claim. Striking out a claim for failure to comply with the CPR requirements was held not to amount to a breach of article 6. Article 6 was not to be construed in a way that disregarded properly considered procedural rules, which ensure that cases come to trial within a reasonable time.

Security in the private rented sector

Challenges by landlords

8.14   Generally the ECtHR has recognised that in deciding the balance between private landlords and tenants a wide margin of appreciation should be applied so that most general challenges to security provisions have failed.[15] This is not to say, however, that in some cases the legal system cannot be so unbalanced as to deprive landlords of their rights.

8.15   In *Scollo v Italy*,[16] the court held that there had been a breach of article 1/1 where the government's eviction policy meant that a disabled landlord who needed his flat for a home found it difficult to evict his tenant who had ceased to pay rent. The problems of obtaining possession in Italy also arose in *Immobiliari Saffi v Italy*[17] where the landlord had obtained possession against the tenant in 1983 but under Italian law which required enforcement of orders to be staggered was unable to obtain possession until 1992. Possession was then further postponed by a legislative intervention. The applicant claimed that there was a breach of article 1/1 and also of article 6(1).

8.16   In upholding the claim, the ECtHR acknowledged that the system of staggering eviction was not of itself a breach of article 1/1. There was, however, a risk that the system could impose an excessive burden on the landlord's ability to dispose of his or her property, and needed safeguards to ensure it did not operate arbitrarily and unforeseeably. The uncertain state the landlord had been left in for eleven years, when he had been unjustly restricted in the use of his property had placed a disproportionate burden on the landlord, and had been a

15 See, for example, *Mellacher v Austria* (1989) 12 EHRR 391, ECtHR and *Spadea and Scalabrino v Italy* (1995) 21 EHRR 482, ECtHR.

16 (1996) 22 EHRR 513, ECtHR.

17 (1999) 30 EHRR 758, ECtHR. See also *CAR Srl v Italy* (1996) 22 EHRR CD 153, ECtHR.

violation of article 1/1. The subsequent intervention of the legislature had also caused undue delay and had deprived the applicant of his right to a fair trial.

8.17   It seems unlikely that this form of delay would occur between possession order and enforcement in England or Wales. More usual is delay due to the imposition of a suspended order for possession. Here, however, even if possession were suspended for a considerable period of time,[18] it seems unlikely that a challenge could be mounted along the lines of *Saffi*, since it is not a problem of enforcing an order made by the court, rather the order is made by the court in those terms after a hearing.

Challenges by tenants

8.18   Where tenants are being evicted by private sector landlords there is much less scope for Convention rights to come into play than when eviction is by a public body. In *Application No 11949/86 v UK*[19] the Commission rejected as inadmissible an application to challenge a forfeiture order which had been made against a long-lease holder, who was in arrears with payments of her service charges. The applicant claimed that she had been deprived of her possessions in breach of the conditions laid down in the second sentence of article 1/1. However, as the state had not deprived the applicant of her flat, nor authorised a third party to do so, the deprivation was not in breach of the rule.

> In view of the exclusively private law relationship between the parties to the lease the Commission considers that the respondent government cannot be responsible by the mere fact that the landlord by its agent, who were private individuals, brought the applicant's lease to an end in accordance with the terms of that lease ...

The fact that the proceedings were brought in a domestic court did not engage state responsibility since the county court merely provided a forum for the determination of the civil right in dispute between the parties.

8.19   The Commission continued:

> It would not appear that the mere fact that an individual was the unsuccessful party to private litigation concerning his tenancy

18 See *Taj v Ali (No 1)* (2001) 33 HLR 26, CA, which emphasised that the period should enable the arrears to be paid off in a reasonable time. Compare with *Lambeth v Henry* (1999) 32 HLR 874, CA.

19 10 EHRR 149, ECtHR.

arrangement with a private landlord could be sufficient to make the state responsible for an alleged violation of article 1/1.

A claim based on breach of article 8 was rejected on grounds of justification.

Assured shorthold tenancies

8.20   Assured shorthold tenancies are primarily used by private sector landlords, but may in some circumstances be used by registered social landlords (particularly when housing households, who have applied to local authorities as homeless under the Housing Act 1996 Part VII[20]). In the private rented sector assured shorthold tenencies are now the majority form of letting. Unlike secure tenancies and fully assured tenancies they offer only limited security of tenure, so that after a minimum six months of the tenancy, provided the necessary notice has been given, the court *must* make an order for possession: HA 1988 s21(4).

8.21   In *Poplar HARCA Ltd v Donoghue*,[21] the Court of Appeal considered whether this mandatory formulation contravened articles 8 and 6 of the Convention. The defendant, who had been found intentionally homeless, was being evicted by her RSL from the property she occupied on an assured shorthold tenancy.

8.22   The court recognised that the eviction did impact on her family life. Accordingly the question was whether it could be justified under art 8(2). The court recognised that:

> this is an area where ... the courts must treat the decisions of Parliament as to what is in the public interest with particular deference. The limited role given to the court under section 21(4) is a legislative policy decision. The correctness of this decision is more appropriate for Parliament than the courts and the HRA does not require the courts to disregard the decision of Parliament in relation to situations of this sort when deciding whether there has been a breach of the Convention.

8.23   Furthermore, the defendant's lack of security was due to her low priority under the legislation because she was found to be intentionally homeless. She was aware from the outset of the temporary nature of the accommodation. For someone in her position (even with children) it was understandable that Parliament would provide an

20 See in particular HA 1996 s209.
21 [2001] EWCA Civ 595; [2001] 3 WLR 183, CA.

expedition procedure to obtain possession, and that the landlord should use the procedure. The defendant also had other remedies she could use (appeal against the intentionality decision, and reference to the ombudsman). Accordingly, section 21(4) did not conflict with her right to family life, nor did it breach article 6, and the court refused to issue a declaration of incompatibility.

Security in the social rented sector

Registered social landlords

8.24   While possession action by local authorities will raise potential for challenges under article 8 and article 1 of the first protocol, if registered social landlords (RSLs) are not considered public bodies, as in some cases they will not[22] then it will be extremely hard to use the Convention in cases where they are seeking to evict their tenants. The arguments applicable to cases brought by clearly private landlords,[23] will be equally applicable to RSLs.

Rent arrears

8.25   One area where a challenge might be considered is where eviction is sought for rent arrears. Depriving someone of their home for a small amount of arrears, might be considered disproportionate,[24] although it seems unlikely that the county court in a discretionary case would order outright possession for a small amount of arrears where the tenant was making an offer of payment. An RSL may, however, rely on the mandatory Ground 8 of Schedule 2 to the Housing Act 1988. As the case of *Application No 11949/86 v UK* illustrates, if an RSL is considered a private body, there is very little scope for intervention, since it is merely relying on its contractual rights.

Warrants for possession

8.26   It is not uncommon for tenants of social landlords to challenge evictions only once a warrant for possession has been issued or indeed

22 See the discussion at para. 13.21.
23 See para. 8.18, above.
24 See *Journal of Housing Law, Possession proceedings and human rights – part 2*, Madge, p21 (Sweet and Maxwell, 2001). Seeking eviction for rent arrears has a legitimate purpose: protection of the rights of others: *Marzari v Italy* (1999) 28 EHRR CD 175, EComHR.

executed. A secure tenant may, before execution, apply for the warrant to be suspended.[25] Where the warrant has been executed it may only be set aside if either it has been obtained by fraud or there has been an abuse of process or oppression in its execution.[26] In the county court, unlike the High Court, the landlord does not have to give the tenant notice that a warrant for possession has been applied for.

8.27   In *St Brice v Southwark LBC*[27] the Court of Appeal considered whether the procedure for issuing warrants for possession was contrary to the Convention. It was held that article 6 did not require an automatic further hearing at the warrant for possession stage. There was no reason why the burden of making an application should not fall upon the person whose rights are in issue, particularly as there had already been a full hearing leading to an order as a result of proceedings initiated by the landlord. Furthermore it was not disproportionate and accordingly not a breach of article 8, for the landlord to seek to enforce the order and for the burden of seeking to prevent the eviction to fall on the tenant, where as here the arrears of rent had grown since the court order and stood in excess of £4,000. There was no breach of article 14 in the different procedures of the High Court and county court.

8.28   Where the tenant does make an application under HA 1985 s85(2) to suspend a warrant for possession, there is no reason why the court should not consider matters not raised at the original trial in deciding how to exercise his or her discretion.[28] Accordingly matters relating for example to the anti-social behaviour of the tenant or his or her family may be raised to resist the warrant being suspended, even though the warrant was obtained on the ground of rent arrears. The discretion to suspend a warrant:

> ... should be used to further the policy of Part IV of the Housing Act 1985, reinforced as it is by article 8 of the European Convention on Human Rights and the Human Rights Act 1998. Accordingly, the courts should bear in mind that that policy is one which involves evicting the tenant from his or her home only after a serious breach of the tenant's obligations has been established, when it is reasonable

25   HA 1985 s85(2). See HA 1988 s9(2) for the equivalent provisions for assured tenants.
26   See most recently *Lambeth LBC v Hughes* (2001) 33 HLR 33, CA, and *Jephson Homes HA v Moisejevs* [2001] 2 All ER 901, CA.
27   [2001] EWCA Civ 1138, CA.
28   *Sheffield CC v Hopkins* [2001] EWCA Civ 1023, CA.

to do so, and the tenant has been proved to have breached any
condition of the [original] order for possession.[29]

Notices to quit by joint tenants

8.29　Service of a notice to quit by a joint tenant is effective to determine a
tenancy.[30] Many local authorities and RSLs encourage the use of such
notices where there has been a relationship breakdown. The effect
of giving notice is often to affect the right to private and family life of
the other tenant under article 8. In *Ure v UK*[31] the Commission
considered that this common law right was justifiable under article
8(2):

> In the present case the Commission notes that the applicant and his
> wife were joint tenants and that, therefore, the right to use the
> apartment was to be exercised by them jointly. The applicant
> apparently was not entitled, under the tenancy agreement, to use the
> flat as a sole tenant. It was therefore clear at the outset that in case
> one of the joint tenants decided to leave, the other could not claim a
> right to become the sole tenant. This was the legal situation as
> regards joint tenancies on all types of property, and not only on
> residential property.
>
> Furthermore, it does not appear that the manner in which the
> authorities balanced the various interests involved, such as the
> interest of the leaving co-tenant, of those in need of accommodation,
> and of the applicant, was arbitrary or unreasonable. Thus, the
> applicant's housing need apparently changed as he was not living
> with his wife and child any more. Moreover, replacement housing
> accommodation had been obtained for the applicant.

Unless much more severe circumstances can be shown, for example,
where the remaining tenant will be rendered homeless, but not in
priority need, a challenge to this practice seems unlikely to succeed.

Succession

8.30　One right which tenants may have, either under the terms of the
tenancy or through statute, is to succession. Generally article 8 cannot

---

29　Per Lord Woolf of Barnes, LCJ, in *Hopkins*, ibid, at para 29.
30　See *Greenwich LBC v McGrady* (1982) 6 HLR 36, CA; *Harrow v Johnstone* (1997)
　　29 HLR 475, HL; *Newlon Housing Trust v Al-Suleiman* (1998) 30 HLR 1132, HL.
31　App No 28027/95, following the decision of the Court of Appeal in *Crawley BC v
　　Ure* [1996] QB 13.

be used to argue that there is a right to succeed to a tenancy. In *S v UK*[32] the lesbian partner of a secure tenant was held not entitled to succeed to her partner's secure tenancy, because she did not fall within the definition of family in HA 1985 s113. The Commission held that there was no breach of article 8 in the local authority land-lord evicting her, since she had no legal entitlement to remain in the property and accordingly it could not be regarded as her 'home'.

8.31   Since the decision in *Fitzpatrick v Sterling Housing Association Ltd,*[33] the rights of Rent Act tenants have diverged from those of assured and secure tenants. In *Fitzpatrick* the House of Lords has held that a same sex partner is capable of being a 'member of the tenant's family' for the purposes of Rent Act 1977 Sch 1. This will strengthen arguments that the limitation of the definition of 'member of the family' in the Housing Act 1985 is in fact discrimina-tory and that the decision in *S v UK* should be revisited.

Owner-occupiers

Mortgagors

8.32   While eviction by a mortgagee undoubtedly interferes with the mortgagor's right to respect for the home, and deprives him or her of his possessions, it will almost always be justifiable. In *Wood v UK,*[34] the Commission said of repossession by a mortgagee:

> In so far as the repossession constituted an interference with the applicant's home the Commission find that this was in accordance with the terms of the loan and the domestic law and was necessary for the protection of the rights and freedoms of others, namely the lender. To the extent that the applicant is deprived of her possessions by repossession, the Commission considers that this deprivation is in the public interest in ensuring payment of contractual debts, and in accordance with the rules provided for by law.

8.33   Furthermore, unless the mortgagee is a public body, such as a local authority, the matter will not engage state powers since the courts are merely enforcing contractual rights between parties in granting an order for possession. Possession may not, however, always be neces-sary for the protection of the rights of the mortgagor. In *Home Loans*

32   (1986) 47 DR 274, EComHR.
33   (1999) 32 HLR 178, HL.
34   See *Wood v UK* (1997) 24 EHRR CD 69, EComHR.

Ltd v Massey[35] possession proceedings were taken against a husband and wife. The husband had no defence to the claim, but the wife did. The county court judge ordered possession against the husband. The Court of Appeal cited article 8 in concluding that this was not an appropriate order, since it was of no benefit to the mortgagee.

8.34   While it is usual that repossession only takes place following a court order, at which the court will consider the provisions of section 36 of the Administration of Justice Act 1970, these provisions do not apply where the mortgagee proceeds by way of peaceable re-entry.[36] It is arguable that the failure to require court proceedings to determine such rights is a breach of article 6.

Relationship breakdown

8.35   Provision for both owner-occupiers and tenants for the readjustment of property rights on matrimonial breakdown are made by the Matrimonial Causes Act 1973 and the Family Law Act 1996. Tenant co-habitees may also make applications under the Family Law Act 1996. For co-habitee owner-occupiers there is, however, no equivalent provision. The use of the constructive or resulting trust will assist un-married couples in many cases, but the court cannot take into account all the circumstances of the case as it can in dividing property on divorce under Matrimonial Causes Act 1973 s25.

8.36   In some cases, differential treatment of married and unmarried persons has been justified by the European Court,[37] but such dis-crimination in relation to the family home is increasingly difficult to justify and in some cases may violate article 8 and article 14.

Leasehold properties

8.37   Where leasehold properties are involved there are likely to be disputes between leaseholders and freeholders. In some circumstances the freeholders may comprise a residents' association which has acquired the building. Residents' associations may also be recognised for the purposes of dealing with a freeholder under the Landlord and Tenant Act 1985. Where associations act in this capacity careful con-sideration will have to be given to their relationship with the tenants,

35 (1997) 29 HLR 902, CA.
36 *Ropaigealach v Barclays Bank plc* (1998) 32 HLR 234, CA.
37 *McMichael v UK* (1995) 20 EHRR 205, ECtHR ; *Smallwood v UK* (1999) 27 EHRR CD 155, EComHR.

and whether, if the tenants disagree with the decisions of the association, they have a right to litigate. In certain circumstances it has been
held that disputes between residents and residents' associations do
not involve a determination of civil rights.[38]

8.38   One undoubted interference with freeholders' property rights is
the enfranchisement rights given to long leaseholders under the
Leasehold Reform Act 1967, and latterly the Landlord and Tenant Act
1987, and the Leasehold Reform, Housing and Urban Development
Act 1993. A challenge to the 1967 Act was made in *James v UK*[39] and
rejected by the ECtHR. Such interference was justified and fell within the wide margin of appreciation which states have in the area of
social policy.

Actions against travellers

8.39   There has been a number of cases before the ECtHR which have involved travellers, partly reflecting increasingly draconian measures
against those who do not live a settled lifestyle. These have related not
only to possession actions but also to the application of planning laws
to the stationing of caravans and the like.[40] In *Chapman* the majority
of the ECtHR upheld the view that there was no positive obligation on
the state to provide sufficient authorised camping sites for travellers.
Furthermore it has been held that the exclusion of sites for gypsies
from the protection of the Mobile Homes Act 1993 is not discriminatory under article 14.[41]

8.40   Where travellers have illegally stationed caravans, landowners
may use possession actions to remove them. Where the landowner is
a private individual or body the provisions of the Convention will not
be engaged.[42] Where the landowner is a public body such as a local
authority, then article 8 will be engaged, since a caravan may consti-

---

38   *Wahlberg, Engman and Engdahl v Sweden* (1983) 15 EHRR CD 79.

39   (1986) Series A No 98; 8 EHRR 123, ECtHR. See also para 3.14, above.

40   See, for example, *Buckley v UK* (1997) 23 EHRR 101, ECtHR and *Chapman v UK*
     (2001) *Times* 30 January, ECtHR. The planning law implications are not
     considered further here, but see Baker, Ed, *Planning Law*, Colville, *Human
     Rights Act 1998: A practitioner's guide'* (Sweet and Maxwell, 1998); *European
     Human Rights Law*, Starmer, Chapter 22 (LAG, 1999).

41   *P v UK* App No 14751/89 (resulting from *Powell v Greenwich LBC* [1989] AC 995,
     HL).

42   See para 8.18, above.

tute a home, if sufficiently established.[43] In most cases it is likely that authorities, particularly if they consider all the needs of the travellers and their family in accordance with Department of the Environment circular 18/94 will be able to justify the eviction. In *R v Brighton and Hove Council ex p Marmont*[44] it was held that where a local authority was using summary proceedings to evict travellers circular 18/94 had no application. Notwithstanding this, given the right to respect for the home, precipitative action without considering the welfare needs of those being evicted might arguably amount to a breach of article 8.

8.41   Authorities may also use the Criminal Justice and Public Order Act 1994 s77 against travellers. This permits authorities to make a direction ordering those living in vehicles on unoccupied land or trespassing on occupied land to leave. Failure to comply with a direction is a criminal offence. The direction may be enforced in the magistrates' court, and it has been held that once the direction is issued there should be as little delay as possible between the giving and enforcing of it.[45]

8.42   In *Ward v Hillingdon LBC*[46] the authority used Criminal Justice and Public Order Act 1994 s77 against a traveller who had moved on to an empty plot on a site for travellers without authorisation. The decision was challenged, among other things, on the basis that forcing him to leave the site was a violation of article 8 as it was disproportionate to the benefit that accrued to the authority. This argument was rejected, and the decision by the authority was justifiable on a number of grounds, including the tension caused on the site by the belief that the applicant had jumped the queue. The court did hold, however, that there was an arguable case for finding that section 77 was incompatible with article 6. As the question of compatibility had not been referred to the Crown, the court decided, however, that it would not be appropriate to consider the question.

Actions against trespassers

8.43   Trespassers may be considered to fall into two groups: so called proper trespassers and 'tolerated trespassers'. The former group may be evicted under summary proceedings in the same way as travellers.

---

43   See cases cited at note 35 above, and para 2.25, above.
44   (1998) 30 HLR 1046, QBD.
45   *R v Wolverhampton MBC ex p Dunne and Rafferty* (1996) 29 HLR 745, QBD.
46   [2001] EWHC Admin 91.

Accordingly article 8 may be engaged on limited occasions as discussed at para 8.40 above. Given that a trespasser by definition has no rights to occupy, it may be argued that article 6 does not apply to any eviction since there are no civil rights to be protected. Accordingly, a state is not required to ensure that there is a right to a court hearing in such cases.

8.44   A tolerated trespasser is an occupier who has remained in occupation after the making of an outright possession order[47] or following breach of a suspended possession order.[48] The trespass is tolerated because the landlord desists from enforcing its rights to evict, and indeed continues to receive rent, however, no new tenancy is created and the occupier's rights in relation to the property are limited.[49] Does the precarious position of tolerated trespassers, and their lack of rights compared to fully secure and assured tenants amount to a lack of respect for the home in breach of article 8? It seems unlikely, the tolerated trespasser is an indulgence, the alternative to which is possession.

> Local authorities and other public housing authorities try to conduct their housing functions as humane and reasonable landlords. In so doing they frequently need to grant indulgences to their tenants to reflect changes in the tenants' circumstances ... if the Court of Appeal decision is correct, the effect of granting the indulgence is to create a new tenancy or licence and the local authority will have to obtain a new possession order. The practical result therefore will be either that the local authority will be reluctant to make reasonable and humane concessions by agreement or in every case will have to make an application to the court to vary the existing order so as to ensure that the old tenancy is not brought to an end. I find it impossible to believe that Parliament intended to produce such an unreasonable regime, penalising sensible agreements out of court and requiring repeated applications to an already overstretched court system.[50]

Given this, it is likely that the position of tolerated trespassers can be justified.

---

47   *Burrows v Brent LBC* (1996) 29 HLR 176, HL.
48   *Greenwich LBC v Regan* (1996) 28 HLR 469, CA.
49   There are no succession rights *Brent LBC v Knightley* (1997) 29 HLR 857, CA, nor are there rights in relation to repair (see para. 10.14, below).
50   Per Lord Browne-Wilkinson in *Burrows*, at p. 173.

Adverse possession

8.45   If a trespasser remains in occupation of a property long enough he or she may acquire rights through the doctrine of adverse possession.[51] In such circumstances the owner of the land who is deprived of possession, may argue that he is deprived of his possessions in a way that it is in breach of article 1/1. In recent cases the Court of Appeal has taken a narrow interpretation of the adverse possession rule to limit the circumstances in which it can be established.[47]

8.46   Notwithstanding this limited interpretation, it may still be the case, that an landowner who is deprived of his property through the operation of the law of adverse possession may wish to challenge the provisions of the Limitation Act 1980, on the basis that the effect is disproportionate and cannot be justified. In *JA Pye (Oxford) Ltd v Graham*,[53] however, the Court of Appeal held that the Limitation Act 1980 does not amount to the deprivation of property or interference with enjoyment of it.

> They deprive a person of his right of access to the courts for the purpose of recovering property, if he has delayed the institution of proceedings for 12 years or more after he has been dispossessed of his land by another person, who has been in adverse possession of it for at least that period. The extinction of the title of the claimant in those circumstances is not a deprivation of possessions or a confiscatory measure for which payment of compensation would be appropriate: it is simply a logical and pragmatic consequence of the barring of his right to bring an action after the expiration of the 'limitation period' (per Mummery LJ at para 52).

8.47   Furthermore, even if the provisions did engage article 1/1, it was held that they were in the public interest:

> Such conditions are reasonably required to avoid the real risk of injustice in the adjudication of stale claims; to ensure certainty of title; and to promote social stability by the protection of the established and peaceable possession of property from the resurrection of old claims. The conditions provided in the 1980 Act are not disproportionate; the period allowed for the bringing of proceedings is reasonable; the conditions are not discriminatory; and they are not impossible, or so excessively difficult, to comply with as to render ineffective the exercise of the legal right of a person, who is

---

51 See Limitation Act 1980 s15(1) and *Asher v Whitlock* (1865) LR 1 QB 1.
52 See, for example, *Bigden v Lambeth LBC* (2001) 33 HLR 43, CA and *Archangel v Lambeth LBC* (2001) 33 HLR 44, CA.
53 [2001] 2 WLR 1293, CA.

entitled to the peaceable enjoyment of his possessions, to recover them from another person, who is alleged to have wrongfully deprived him of them (per Mummery LJ at para 52).

CHAPTER 9

Anti-social behaviour

Introduction

9.1 Anti-social behaviour has become a key issue for social landlords,[1] and a range of different legal actions is now available against alleged perpetrators of such behaviour. Each of these will be considered in turn, together with possible challenges under the Convention. A number of cases relating to anti-social behaviour have already raised claims under the Convention, and these are considered below. It may be noted at this point, however, that the courts have generally been sympathetic to the government and landlords when faced with such claims and have refused to cut down the powers that have been granted to deal with the problem.

Eviction

9.2 Tenants living in social housing generally have security of tenure either as secure tenants under the Housing Act (HA) 1985 or assured tenants under the Housing Act (HA) 1988, and an application for possession requires proof of a ground for possession. In relation to nuisance cases two grounds are generally relied upon:

- Breach of tenancy agreement (ground 1, HA 1985; ground 12, HA 1988[2]).
- Specific nuisance ground (ground 2, HA 1985; ground 14, HA 1988[3]).

9.3 The nuisance ground was amended by HA 1996 for both types of tenancies and is now in the following terms:

> The tenant or a person residing in or visiting the dwelling-house –
> (a) has been guilty of conduct causing or likely to cause a nuisance or annoyance to a person residing, visiting or otherwise engaging in lawful activity in the locality, or
> (b) has been convicted of –
> (i) using the dwelling-house or allowing it to be used for immoral or illegal purposes, or

---

1 See also the government response to the issue, which has led to much of the new legislation discussed in the chapter, *Anti-social Behaviour on Housing Estates: Consultation Paper on Probationary Tenancies,* Department of the Environment, (DoE London, 1995) and *Report of Policy Action Team 8: Anti-social Behaviour,* Social Exclusion Unit, (Stationery Office London, 2000).
2 HA 1985 Sch 2 Part I; HA 1988 Sch 2 Part II.
3 HA 1985 Sch 2 Part I; HA 1988 Sch 2 Part II.

(ii) an arrestable offence committed in, or in the locality of, the dwelling-house.

9.4   Both grounds for possession are discretionary, ie, before the judge can order possession he or she must be satisfied that it is 'reasonable to make the order'.[4] In either case, even if the judge considers it reasonable to grant possession s/he may suspend the order on terms, for example, of on-going good behaviour.[5]

9.5   Given that eviction will deprive the tenant of their home, issues relating to article 8 have been raised in possession cases. Two particular issues need to be considered:

- Is an outright order justified?
- Should eviction be granted for the behaviour of others?

Is an outright order justified?

9.6   In *Lambeth LBC v Howard*[6] Sedley LJ considered in detail the impact of HRA 1998 on possession claims under ground 2. As possession was an interference with the right to respect under article 8(1) the question was always whether the interference was justified in accordance with article 8(2). This required consideration of whether the interference was necessary in a democratic society for the protection of the rights and freedoms of others. The proper approach to this was that taken by Longmore J in *Johns and Maclellan*:[7]

> Necessary in a democratic society does not mean indispensable; nor does it mean desirable. Convention jurisprudence has decided that it means:
> (a) that the reasons given to justify the interference must be relevant and sufficient;
> (b) that the interference must correspond to a pressing social need; and
> (c) that the interference must be proportionate to the aim pursued ...

9.7   Sedley LJ continued:

> As this court has said more than once, there is nothing in article 8, or in the associated jurisprudence of the European Court of Human Rights, which should carry county courts to materially different

---

4   HA 1985 s84(2); HA 1988 s7(4).
5   HA 1985 s85(2),(3); HA 1988 s9(2), (3).
6   (2001) 33 HLR 58, CA.
7   *R (on the application of Johns and McLellan) v Bracknell Forest DC* (2001) 33 HLR 45, QBD, see further para 9.19, below.

outcomes from those that they have been arriving at for many years when deciding whether it is reasonable to make an outright or a suspended or no possession order. Nevertheless, as the judge in the present case has demonstrated in the final passage of his judgment, it can do no harm, and may often do a great deal of good, if the exercise is approached for what it is, an application of the principle of proportionality.

Accordingly, the conclusion of the county court judge that outright (rather than suspended) possession was appropriate in this case was upheld.

Eviction for the behaviour of others

9.8   The expanded nuisance ground permits the eviction of a tenant for the behaviour of a person residing in or visiting the tenant. In *Portsmouth CC v Bryant,*[8] Sedley LJ commented that following the Human Rights Act 1998 coming into force, the courts might have to reconsider whether it is appropriate to have 'strict liability' of tenants for the conduct of others and whether a tenant can be said to have 'allowed' conduct by failing to prevent it. It should be noted that the other judges did not agree with Sedley LJ.

9.9   In *Castle Vale HAT v Gallagher,*[9] article 8 was used to justify the making of a suspended rather than an outright order where the perpetrator was the tenant's daughter and her boyfriend, who were now moving out because the daughter had bought a house. However, given the comments of Sedley LJ in the case of *Lambeth LBC v Howard* it seems unlikely that the Convention is likely to effect a major shift in outcomes in such cases.

Representation at possession hearings

9.10   Many landlords seek to have anti-social behaviour cases heard within very short time periods, and the courts have often granted applications for quick service of documents and early hearing dates. This may, however, considerably disadvantage tenants if they are unable to obtain legal aid to defend the case.

8   (2000) 32 HLR 906. See also his comments in *Gallagher* (note 9, below), at para 52.
9   [2001] EWCA Civ 944; April 2001 *Legal Action* 20. Sedley LJ reiterated at para 50 that consideration of whether orders are proportionate does not 'introduce anything novel into the way the courts for many years have approached this question'.

9.11   In *Bates v Croydon LBC*[10] legal aid had not been determined by the time the directions hearing came before the court on an application for possession for anti-social behaviour. The tenant appeared un-represented and sought an adjournment, which was refused. Very tight time-limits were imposed, with only three days for the tenant to consider the landlord's evidence and serve a response.

9.12   At trial the tenant was still unrepresented and renewed her appli-cation for an adjournment, which was again refused. An outright pos-session order was made. Having obtained representation, the tenant appealed against the refusals to grant adjournments. On appeal to the Court of Appeal, it was held that adjournments should have been granted as representation was likely to make a substantial difference to the outcome of the case. Citing *Airey v Ireland*[11] the court held that where a trial entailed emotional involvement or depended materially on the credibility of witnesses, representation by an advocate would be a considerable benefit, especially where legal aid was in principle available.

Injunctions

9.13   An injunction may be sought to prevent anti-social behaviour. The primary cause of action on which injunctive relief may be claimed is for breach of contract. In such a case the injunction will be sought against the tenant or tenants. As such it is a fairly straightforward remedy, and is unlikely to raise any issues under the Convention.

9.14   The fact that injunctions could only realistically be sought against tenants,[12] who may not be the main perpetrators of anti-social behav-iour, led to a change in the law in HA 1996. Section 152 of the 1996 Act permits local housing authorities and housing action trusts to seek injunctions against both tenants and non-tenants, in circum-stances of actual violence or threats of violence being made. Given the limitations on when they can be granted, it seems unlikely that the principle of granting injunctions in these circumstances could be open to challenge.

9.15   Once the court has decided that an injunction should be made, the terms of the injunction may prevent the defendant 'from entering

---

10 [2001] EWCA Civ 134; [2001] JHL D32, CA.

11 (1979) Series A No 32.

12 Although a number of local authorities did seek (experimentally) to obtain injunctions on the basis of the Local Government Act 1972 s222, the legality of these was never fully tested.

residential premises to which this section applies or being found in the locality of such premises'.[13] Thus defendants may be banned from a particular area. This may give rise to potential challenges to the terms of injunctions if a defendant feels that his rights to respect to family and private life and the home have been unduly interfered with.

9.16   This raises similar issues to those concerning the terms of anti-social behaviour orders, and for the reasons set out in para 9.33, below, it seems unlikely that a challenge on this basis would have a great chance of success.

9.17   An injunction under HA 1996 s152 may have a power of arrest attached to it (s152(6)). By HA 1996 s153 a power of arrest may also be attached to an injunction against a tenant of a local authority or registered social landlord, in cases involving violence or threats of violence. It has been suggested[14] that the power of arrest which may be attached to injunctions against tenants in public housing but not other occupiers may be an arbitrary discrimination and violation of article 5 (right to liberty) and article 14. Given the conclusion of the court in relation to differentiation of treatment for introductory tenants[15] it seems unlikely that discrimination would be found. Furthermore, the arrest for breach of the injunction is hedged with legal safeguards such that the requirements of lawful detention under article 5 would be fulfilled.

Introductory tenancies

9.18   The Housing Act 1996 introduced a new form of tenancy to be used by local housing authorities and housing action trusts: the introductory tenancy. Where an authority adopts an introductory tenancy regime, all new tenants are for the first 12 months of the tenancy 'introductory'. Effectively this means they may be evicted without the landlord having to prove any grounds for possession in the county court nor that it is reasonable to grant possession, provided that the landlord has served a proper notice on the tenant which must offer an internal review of the decision to evict, and has, if requested, carried out such a review.[16]

---

13 HA 1996 s152(1)(c).

14 See *Journal of Housing Law, Housing Law and the Human Rights Act 1998*, Alder p67 (Sweet and Maxwell, 1999).

15 See para 9.24, below.

16 See Housing Act 1996 ss127–129.

9.19   The compatibility of introductory tenancies with the Convention was considered in *R (on the application of Johns and McLellan) v Bracknell Forest DC*.[17] The case was brought by two introductory tenants, one of whom the authority was seeking to evict due to nuisance behaviour and the other due to rent arrears. It was argued on behalf of the tenants that introductory tenancies were incompatible with articles 6 and 8. Longmore J held that both articles had been engaged by the action taken by the authority.

9.20   In relation to article 6, however, Longmore J held that although the internal review was not of itself by an independent and impartial tribunal, this was not fatal. The judge continued that the internal reviewer in such cases fell within the principles of *Bryan v UK*[18] where appeal from a planning inspector to the High Court was held to constitute an appeal to a court with full jurisdiction, and accordingly comply with article 6.[19] Thus in principle the eviction process for introductory tenancies was compatible with article 6.

9.21   The court left open, however, whether in a particular case a landlord may have acted, in the conduct of the internal review, in a way that is incompatible with article 6, for example, by refusing to disclose sources of evidence. In such a case it may well be possible to argue the article 6 point on a judicial review of the authority's decision to evict, although Longmore J noted that in some cases withholding sources of information may be justified.[20]

9.22   Although holding that article 8 was engaged by the eviction proceedings, the judge concluded that they were obviously in accordance with the law (as laid down in HA 1996). The key question was whether the interference was necessary in a democratic society for the protection of the rights and freedoms of others. Pointing to the need to take swift action to protect neighbours from nuisance and to prevent rent arrears impacting on tenants who did pay their rent showed that the interference was relevant, sufficient and corresponded to a pressing social need. Thus neither the statutory scheme itself nor the decision by a local authority to adopt it were incompatible with article 8. In reaching this conclusion Longmore J emphasised the wide margin of appreciation national legislatures have in the area of housing policy.

9.23   It was also argued on behalf of the tenants that introductory

---

17 (2001) 33 HLR 45, QBD, currently pending appeal.

18 (1995) 21 EHRR 342.

19 See *Albert and Le Compte v Belgium* (1983) 5 EHRR 533, ECtHR and para 4.28, above.

20 See, eg, *Fitt v UK* (2000) 30 EHRR 480, ECtHR; *Rowe and Davis v UK* (2000) 30 EHRR 1, ECtHR; and *R v Joe Smith* (2000) *Times* 20 December.

tenancies were not a proportional response. This argument was also dismissed, the judge pointing to the requirements for reasons to be given by the landlord, and the fact that the introductory tenancy lasted only 12 months. Although the legislation did not require land-lords to have regard to necessity and proportionality in deciding to evict, the judge concluded that 'there is no reason to suppose that in any given case the council would not so have regard. If they did not, the remedy of judicial review is available ...'.

9.24   Finally a number of points were made in relation to article 14, for instance, that introductory tenancies were discriminatory. The judge ruled out any comparison with tenants who have a different status as giving rise to any discrimination. He also briefly and without full argument ruled out any question of discrimination on the basis of geography, and the fact that some authorities had adopted introduc-tory tenancy schemes and others not.

9.25   Subject to any decision on appeal in this case, the introductory tenancy regime can be said to be compatible with the Convention. However, the way that landlords apply it in any individual case may give rise to arguments about a fair hearing and proportionality.

Pets

9.26   Many social landlords have policies about the keeping of pets. Breach of such policies may lead to the landlord seeking possession or alter-natively an injunction requiring removal of the pet. Policies banning pets in themselves are unlikely to be a breach of article 8. In *Artingstoll v UK*[21] a complaint made under article 8 about a council policy which prohibited the keeping of small dogs and cats as pets in a sheltered housing scheme, was held inadmissible. Relying on earlier juris-prudence it was held that the keeping of pets is not within the sphere of private life, and accordingly does not fall within article 8. Further-more, the Council's policy was made clear to the tenant when he entered into the lease.

9.27   If a tenant were required to remove a pet by injunction, even if it were not a breach of article 8, it could be argued that it is a breach of article 1/1. However, an injunction is a discretionary remedy and the balancing act required by article 1/1 would almost certainly be carried out. If possession is sought, prompting a claim of breach of articles 8 and 1/1 it is likely that if the judge has properly considered

21   (1995) 19 EHRR CD 92.

the reasonableness of granting possession (and it is likely that an order would be suspended on condition that the pet is removed) then it is unlikely that there would be any breach of the Convention.

Anti-social behaviour orders

9.28 The anti-social behaviour order contained in the Crime and Disorder Act 1998 is not, strictly speaking a 'housing' provision. It can be applied to perpetrators of anti-social behaviour in any location, and is not dependant on whether or not they are occupiers of any particular type of housing.

9.29 Applications for an anti-social behaviour order may be made by either a local authority or the police where it is considered that the defendant has behaved in 'a manner that caused or was likely to cause harassment alarm or distress and an order is necessary to protect people in [the area] from further acts': Crime and Disorder Act 1998 s1(1).

Criminal or civil?

9.30 Applications for an order are made to the magistrates court, sitting in a civil capacity. In *R v Manchester Crown Court ex p McCann*[22] the Court of Appeal upheld a Divisional Court ruling that applications for an anti-social behaviour order were correctly classified as civil in nature. Accordingly it is only the provisions of article 6(1) and not 6(2) and (3)[23] which apply to such proceedings.

Hearsay evidence

9.31 Because an application for an anti-social behaviour order is a civil matter, the use of hearsay evidence is permitted, although subject to the provisions of the Civil Evidence Act 1995. This might seem to contravene the requirement for a 'fair and public hearing', however, the ECtHR has held that article 6 does not always mean that a statement from a witness must always be made in court and in public.[24]

---

22 [2001] 1 WLR 358, CA.
23 See para 1.101, above.
24 *X v UK* (1987)15 EHRR CD 113, ECtHR. See also *Fitt v UK* (2000) 30 EHRR 480, ECtHR; *Rowe and Davis v UK* (2000) 30 EHRR 1, ECtHR.

Indeed in *Doorson v Netherlands*[25] the Court stressed that 'the admissibility of evidence is primarily a matter for regulations by national law and as a general rule it is for national courts to assess the evidence before them ...'

9.32   The use of hearsay evidence in an application for anti-social behaviour orders was considered in *R v Marylebone Magistrates' Court, ex p Clingham.*[26] The authority which applied for the order sought to call evidence from police officers regarding complaints made to the police about the defendant by other persons who were neither to be identified nor called to give evidence. A notice was served pursuant to the Magistrates' Court (Hearsay Evidence in Civil Proceedings) Rules 1999.[27] An application for judicial review of the admissibility of the evidence was rejected. The use of hearsay evidence in these circumstances was not a breach of article 6, given it would be for the court to decide what weight to give to the evidence or whether it was probative.

The terms of the order

9.33   Once it has been established that a defendant has acted in the requisite manner for an order to be made, the magistrates' court may 'make an order...which prohibits the defendant from doing anything described in the order' (Crime and Disorder Act 1998 s1(4)). Section 1(6) of the Act states that 'The prohibitions that may be imposed ... are those necessary for the purpose of protecting [persons] from further anti-social acts ...'

9.34   The breadth of this power may on occasion raise potential challenges to the orders which are made, if, for example, they disproportionately limit a defendant's access to his home or family. However, it seems likely that such orders will have to be extremely draconian before any challenge is likely to succeed.

9.35   Where a person has been excluded from an area, and can no longer visit his or her family, he or she may seek to rely on article 8. However in *McCullough v UK*,[28] a challenge to a ban on an alleged terrorist from visiting mainland Britain from Northern Ireland[29] the Commission doubted that there was such an interference since it was not established that the applicant's mother or brother could not visit

---

25   (1996) 22 EHRR 330, ECtHR.
26   (2001) EWCH Admin 1, Divisional Court.
27   SI No 681.
28   (1977) 25 EHRR CD 34, ECtHR.
29   Under the Prevention of Terrorism Act 1974.

him. Article 8 does not confer a general right to reside in or move to any particular part of a Convention territory.

9.36   In *Anderson et al v UK*,[30] allegations of nuisance were made against a number of young people who were subsequently banned from a shopping centre. They sought to challenge the legality of the ban under article 11 (the right to peaceful assembly). It was held that article 11 does not include the right to pass and re-pass in public places or to assemble for purely social purposes anywhere one wishes.

Evidence collection and information sharing

9.37   For local authorities and registered social landlords wishing to achieve success in legal cases against alleged perpetrators of anti-social behaviour, the collection of evidence may be crucial. Evidence once collected may be shared with others, or indeed cases may be based on evidence that has been passed on from others, for example, the police. The sharing of information may also be the basis of decisions to exclude applicants from being allocated housing.[31]

9.38   Where information has been collected secretly, for example, through listening devices right to privacy issues may be raised. Secret listening devices may invade privacy contrary to article 8.[32] The Regulation of Investigatory Powers Act (RIPA) 2000 seeks to put covert surveillance by public authorities[33] on a legitimate footing. Covert surveillance will be lawful if authorised in accordance with the Act.[34] Where a local authority carries out covert surveillance, authorisation may be provided by an assistant chief officer or an officer responsible for the management of an investigation.[35] When authorising covert surveillances the officer must be satisfied that the authorisation is

30 (1997) 25 EHRR 172, ECtHR.
31 See para 7.21, above.
32 For example, *Khan v UK* (2000) *Times* 23 May. See also *Tsaviachidis v Greece* (1999) 27 EHRR CD 27.
33 This will include any local authority within the meaning of Local Government Act 1999 s1, but not registered social landlords, see RIPA 2000 Sch 1.
34 RIPA 2000 s27. This does not, however, make covert surveillance which is not authorised unlawful, but does ensure that 'the action is carried out in accordance with the law and subject to stringent safeguards against abuse. It will also make the action less vulnerable to challenge under the Human Rights Act 1998', *Code of Practice on Covert Surveillance*, para 2.1, (issued by the Home Secretary under s71 of the Act).
35 The Regulation of Investigatory Powers Act (Prescription of Offices, Ranks and Positions) Order 2000 SI No 2417.

necessary on one of the specified grounds[36] and the surveillance is proportionate to what is sought to be achieved in carrying it out.[37]

9.39   Information may be disclosed by the police to local authorities or RSLs under Crime and Disorder Act 1998 ss5 and 6. Human rights issues are likely to be relevant when information is sought by a local authority from another authority or from the police, as it may give rise to a claim that the respect to private life has been breached. In these circumstances it may be important to distinguish between information which is in the public domain (for example, a criminal conviction or an order for possession) and allegations kept on file which have not been subject to a court decision.

9.40   In a different context, in *R v A local authority in the Midlands ex p LM*,[38] Dyson J considered the effect of article 8 in respect of disclosure of information regarding allegations of sexual abuse. He held that the information should only be disclosed if there was a 'pressing need' to do so, and that the police and social services department had failed to apply the correct test. In *MS v Sweden*[39] an applicant's medical records were passed to the social insurance office to determine a claim for compensation. It was held that there was no violation of article 8 because the interference had a legitimate aim and was necessary in a democratic society. It is likely that in cases of anti-social behaviour a similar justification could be mounted.

Duties to victims

9.41   On the other side of the coin, a failure to act to prevent anti-social behaviour may leave authorities vulnerable to legal proceedings from the victims. Failure to provide peaceful enjoyment of the home may amount to a breach of article 8.[40]

9.42   In the context of a failure to take action in relation to complaints of anti-social behaviour (including racist attacks) the English courts have held that there is no remedy against a local authority landlord.

36 In the case of anti-social behaviour the grounds most likely to be relied upon are that the surveillance is necessary for the purpose of preventing or detecting crime or of preventing disorder, in the interests of public safety or occasionally for the purpose of protecting public health.

37 RIPA 2000 s28.

38 [2000] COD 41, QBD.

39 (1997) 28 EHRR 313, ECtHR.

40 See para 2.40.

In *Hussain v Lancaster CC*[41] the local authority had neither been negligent in failing to use any of its powers to prevent the behaviour, nor had there been a nuisance for which the authority could be said to be liable. The nuisance argument was rejected on two grounds. First, to amount to nuisance the acts concerned must involve the alleged perpetrators using their land to create it. In this case the acts took place in the street or on the victim's land. Secondly, for the local authority to be liable they must as landlord have authorised or adopted the nuisance. This they had not done.

9.43 More recently in *Mowan v Wandsworth LBC*[42] the Court of Appeal confirmed the decision in *Hussain*. The claimant was the long lease-holder of a flat owned by the authority, the first defendant in the case. The upstairs flat was let to the second defendant under a secure tenancy. The second defendant had severe mental health problems and caused a significant nuisance to the claimant, who issued proceedings against both the authority and the second defendant. The authority sought to have the proceedings against them struck out and such an order was duly made. On appeal it was argued that the courts should re-interpret the earlier law in order not to leave the claimant without a remedy to protect her from the breach of article 8.

9.44 The argument was rejected. It was not clear that the claimant did not have an effective remedy. She might succeed in her action against the second defendant,[43] further judicial review of the authority's decisions might be open to the claimant. Nor did the fact that the local authority owed no duty of care in such cases amount to an exclusionary rule contrary to article 6,[44] since that applies where an applicant has a cause of action, but is prevented from exercising by an exclusionary rule preventing its application to a particular type of defendant.

9.45 *Mowan* does not amount to a full consideration of the application of the Convention in these circumstances, as it was based on facts that occurred prior to HRA 1998 coming into force. The Court of Appeal was accordingly not able to consider whether the failure to take any action by the authority was a direct breach of article 8. It is understood that the claimant intends to bring a new action based on facts occurring after 2 October 2000.

---

41 (1999) 31 HLR 164. Compare with *Lippiatt v South Gloucestershire DC* (1999) 31 HLR 1114.

42 (2001) 33 HLR 56.

43 The evidence was not such as to convince the court that her mental incapacity meant that no injunction could be granted against her.

44 See *Osman v UK* (2000) 29 EHRR 245, ECtHR.

CHAPTER 10

Housing conditions

10.1   The conditions that occupiers live in give rise to a number of issues, which need to be differentiated between those where the occupier lives in private sector housing and those where the occupier lives in local authority housing.

Positive duties

10.2   The question of whether there are positive duties on the state to intervene to maintain housing conditions and indeed to protect against nuisance and interference with an occupier's enjoyment of the home is one which the ECtHR has considered on a number of occasions.

10.3   In general, the law in England and Wales provides a large number of safeguards for occupiers of property. In addition to the common law tort of nuisance, tenants are particularly protected against their landlords. In the case of short tenancies (ie, those of less than seven years), the Landlord and Tenant Act 1985 s11 implies into the lease a repairing obligation on the landlord. Furthermore the Housing Act 1985 and the Environmental Protection Act 1990 provide local authorities with an array of powers which they can use against landlords, and indeed owner-occupiers, who fail to keep their properties in an adequate condition.

10.4   These provisions generally provide a comprehensive system of protection for people in their homes. Nonetheless it must be remembered that a failure to protect may be a breach of article 8. Cases of severe environmental pollution may interfere with an occupier's enjoyment of his or her home and require the interference of the state to prevent it.[1] The cases where the ECtHR has imposed a positive duty have been ones of severe interference. In some circumstances the lack of protection from interference can be justified. In *Hunter v Canary Wharf Ltd*[2] the House of Lords held that occupiers of homes did not have a claim in nuisance arising out of development of the London Docklands area. A case was pursued before the Commission, who ruled it inadmissible.[3] The redevelopment of the Docklands area, providing an essential link road, justified the dust nuisance lasting

1   *Powell and Rayner v UK* (1990) 12 EHRR 355, ECtHR (noise pollution from Heathrow Airport); *Lopez Ostra v Spain* (1995) 20 EHRR 277 ECtHR (smells, fumes and noise from waste-treatment plant); and *Guerra v Italy* (1998) 26 EHRR 357, ECtHR (toxic emissions from a factory). See further para 2.41, above.

2   [1997] AC 655, HL.

3   *Khatun v UK* (1998) 26 EHRR CD 212, EComHR.

some three and a half years caused to occupiers living by the development.

10.5   Accordingly, it is only if a major gap in legal protection can be identified, having a disproportionate effect on occupiers, will the Convention come into play. One area where it might be considered that there is a gap is in relation to certain types of noise nuisance. In particular it has been held that the Environmental Protection Act 1990 does not cover nuisance from vehicles.[4] In cases where poor sound insulation means that all noises can be heard from an adjoining property it has also been held that there is no liability at common law on the part of the landlord.[5]

Housing conditions in the private sector

10.6   Unless positive obligations are imposed on the state to intervene to protect housing conditions (see above para 10.2), then private sector tenants will have no additional remedies provided by the Convention to those already existing at private law, which enables them to take action against their landlords, since the matter will be one relating to the contractual relationship between two private parties.

Action against property owners

10.7   From the point of view of the owner of property, however, the powers of local authorities to intervene to require works to be carried out to his or her property,[6] to prevent its use for certain purposes,[7] to require demolition[8] and in some circumstances to compulsorily acquire them may seem draconian, and certainly on the face of it a breach of article 1/1. If the powers are exercised against an owner-occupier they may also be a breach of article 8.

10.8   The fact that a wide margin of appreciation to states is permitted in this area is illustrated by *Howard v UK*.[9] The home of the applicants, two elderly brothers, was compulsorily purchased under the powers in the Town and Country Planning Act 1971. The brothers

---

4   *Haringey LBC v Jowett* (1999) 32 HLR 308, QBD.
5   *Southwark LBC v Mills; Baxter v Camden LBC* (1999) 32 HLR 148, HL. It is arguable, however, that there is a liability under the Environmental Protection Act 1990 if it can be shown that the state of the premises is 'prejudicial to health'.
6   HA 1985 s189.
7   HA 1985 s264.
8   HA 1985 s265.
9   (1985) 52 DR 198.

argued that the purchase was a breach of both articles 8 and 1/1. The Commission applied the same approach to whether the action was justified for both articles, ie, that:

> the competent authorities struck a fair balance between the rights of the individual property owner and the rights of the community, in any expropriation of the property. A significant factor in any such balance will be the availability of compensation, reflecting the value of the property expropriated.

10.9   In confirming the purchase which had been upheld following a public inquiry, the balance had been struck since:

- the interference was in accordance with law under a clear statutory enactment;
- the inspector's report had expressly addressed whether or not the applicants' particular property should be included within the order;
- the inspector balanced the advantage of the exclusion of the property against the disadvantage to the community as a whole, namely that certain sheltered housing would not be built or would be rendered substantially more expensive;
- the applicants were offered alternative suitable residential accommodation in the immediate vicinity; and
- the applicants were entitled to full compensation.[10]

10.10   Accordingly, the statutory provisions which allow for the intervention of the state to deal with poor property conditions are unlikely to be subject to a successful claim for breach of article 1/1.

Local authority tenants

10.11   A number of particular issues arise in relation to local authority tenants.

Unfitness provisions and condensation dampness

10.12   While the Housing Act 1985 makes extensive provision to deal with unfit properties, the provisions cannot be enforced by a local authority in relation to their own property.[11]

---

10 On compensation see also *Ceskomoravska Myslivecka Jednota v Czech Republic* (1999) 28 EHRR CD 152 and para 3.16, above.

11 *R v Cardiff CC ex p Cross* (1981) 6 HLR 6, CA.

10.13 This may leave a gap in protection in relation particularly to condensation dampness. The Landlord and Tenant Act 1985 s11 does not cover condensation dampness which arises due to a design defect and is not affecting the structure and exterior of the building.[12] While a remedy may be available under the Environmental Protection Act 1990 s82 it can be argued that this may not be effective as there is no legal aid available to pursue such a claim and any compensation is limited.[13] It may be argued therefore that the state does not provide adequate protection for local authority tenants living in this situation. Furthermore, if a local authority fails to take action to deal with severe conditions a direct claim could be made against it under HRA 1998 s6.

Tolerated trespassers

10.14 The particular position of tolerated trespassers may also be considered. The status of such occupiers is considered in para 8.47, above. A tolerated trespasser does have the right to sue in nuisance,[14] however, there will be no contractual obligation on the landlord to repair.[15] If the tolerated trespasser's tenancy is revived retrospectively the repairing obligation will also be revived, but the tenant is not automatically entitled to have such an order made.[16]

10.15 Can this lack of protection, for an occupier who may be in occupation for a number of years be justified? Given the arguments which can be used to justify the lack of security for such occupiers,[17] presumably the same arguments could also be used to justify the lack of repairing obligations (although perhaps it is harder to justify the lack of repairing obligations than security, but this would seem to follow from a decision that there is no contractual relationship between the parties).

---

12 *Quick v Taff Ely DC* [1986] QB 809, CA.
13 It is understood that a challenge to the limitation of HA 1985 s11 based on article 8 of the Convention will be heard by the Court of Appeal in autumn 2001.
14 *Pemberton v Southwark LBC* (2000) 32 HLR 784, CA.
15 *Lambeth LBC v Rogers* (1999) 32 HLR 361, CA.
16 *Marshall v Bradford MDC* [2001] EWCA 594, CA.
17 See para 8.47.

CHAPTER 11

Support for housing costs

11.1   The state provides for support for housing costs through a number of means: housing benefit for tenants on low incomes; income support to cover mortgage costs for home-owners on benefits; and more generally (although now for an increasingly small number of tenants) by rent control under the Rent Act 1977.

11.2   It is difficult to argue that there is any obligation on the state arising from article 8 to provide a certain level of benefits or affordability. Given the current lack of a right to a home[1] it cannot be argued that article 8 imposes an obligation on the state to provide an *affordable* home. In the context of rights to benefits to guarantee respect for family life it has been said that:

> ... it remains open for the limits of the protection under article 8 to be explored in the context of entitlements to social security. But it would be fair to say that there are few indications that the Strasbourg authorities regard the Convention right here as including an obligation on the state to make payments to families for their support.[2]

11.3   In *Painter*[2a] Lightman J at para 16, accepted that a concession that the refusal of housing benefit cannot amount to a breach of article 8 was rightly made. He continued, however, that by the grant of housing benefit the UK had demonstrated respect for the home. Accordingly in the operation of the housing benefit scheme articles 8 and 14 are engaged, and it may be challenged on the basis that it is not compliant with the Convention. Accordingly, the provision of benefits does raise a number of issues which may be considered, as does the imposition of rent controls.

Provision of benefits

Withdrawals and reduction of benefits

11.4   Reduction and limitation in benefits has been a regular feature of government policy over the past 20 years. In particular housing benefit payments have been reduced for young single people by the single room rent requirement and for all claimants in private rented

---

1   See para 2.5, above.

2   See *Human Rights Act 1998: A practitioner's guide*, Baker, *Social Security*, White, (Sweet and Maxwell, 1998), para 12.30.

2a   *R (on the application of Painter) v Carmarthenshire CC HBRB; R (on the application of Murphy) v Westminster CC* [2001] EWHC Admin 308.

housing by the imposition of rent ceilings.[3] Such restrictions have been applied prospectively, so that existing claimants have been protected provided they remain in the same property. For owner-occupiers benefits have also been withdrawn, so that mortgage interest is no longer paid on the first nine months of any claim.

11.5   Given both the lack of an obligation on the state to support families, and the margin of appreciation which even if there were such an obligation would be given to states, it seems unlikely that prospective changes in benefits will be challengeable under article 8. Careful consideration should be given, however, to their impact on individuals, and in particular to the protection given by the transitional provisions.

Delays in payments

11.6   Delays in payment of housing benefit by some local authorities have now become notorious. Delays in making payments could give rise to claims under both article 8 and article 1/1. Failure to make a payment to which an applicant is entitled has been held in *Gaygusuz v Austria*[4] to be a pecuniary right for the purposes of article 1/1. The ECtHR did not need to go on to consider a claim whether the failure to pay emergency assistance was also a breach of article 8, but a failure to pay housing benefit so that eviction follows could clearly be framed as a lack of respect for family life and the home.

11.7   In circumstances where delays lead to loss of the home it is unlikely that any civil action under common law would be successful, however, applicants in such a case may wish to consider an action under HRA 1998 s6.

Appeals procedures

11.8   As social security benefits are considered a 'civil right',[5] the provisions of article 6 must be complied with in any adjudication procedure. This has led to particular reform of housing benefit review boards, which, given that the decision makers (local authority councillors)

---

3   See the Housing Benefit (General) Regulations 1987 SI No 1971 reg 11 and the Rent Officers (Housing Benefits Functions) Order 1997 SI No 1984.

4   (1997) 23 EHRR 364, ECtHR.

5   See *Feldbrugge v The Netherlands* (1986) Series A No 99; 8 EHRR 425, ECtHR; *Deumeland v Germany* (1986) Series A No 100, 8 EHRR 448, ECtHR; *Salesi v Italy* (1993) Series A No 257–E, ECtHR; and *Schuler-Zgraggen v Switzerland* (1993) Series A No 263; 16 EHRR 405, ECtHR.

were from the authority which decided the claim, failed to provide an 'independent and impartial' tribunal. From 2 July 2001 housing benefit appeals will be heard by the Appeals Service.

11.9   Notwithstanding these changes it has been suggested that there may be circumstances where article 6 may still be breached. In particular, there may be unreasonable delays, 'public hearings' may be limited, and there may not be equality of arms between the parties.[6]

Discrimination

11.10   As noted above, in *Painter*[7] it was held that the operation of the housing benefits system did engage Convention rights and therefore could be in breach of those rights if it operated in a discriminatory manner. The complaint in *Painter* related to regulation 7 of the Housing Benefit (General) Regulations 1987[8] which defines those persons who are not to be treated as liable to make payments in respect of a dwelling and are accordingly not entitled to benefit. They include at paragraph 1(c)(i) those whose liability arises under an agreement with a former partner and is in respect of a dwelling which the claimant and his or her former partner occupied before they ceased to be partners. In *Painter*, the claimant had been in receipt of housing benefit in respect of a room in his landlady's house. He formed a relationship with his landlady and they cohabited. When the relationship came to an end, he remained living in the house and claimed housing benefit. This was refused under regulation 7(1)(c).

11.11   Although Lightman J held that articles 8 and 14 of the Convention were engaged, he nonetheless rejected the claim that the claimant was being discriminated against compared to tenants who had not had a relationship with their landlord. He recognised at paragraph 18 of the judgment that:

> ... the need of the secretary of state to make a difficult choice on a pressing social problem between allowing a scheme to continue which was the occasion for abuse and occasioned the most serious practical difficulties for local authorities and the courts and tribunals or adopt a new scheme which would effectively preclude many (if not all) of the occasions for abuse at the cost of requiring claimants on

6   See further *Journal of Housing Law, Housing Benefit Appeals and the Human Rights Act*, Rahilly, (Sweet and Maxwell, 2001).

7   See note 2a, above. See also *Tucker v Secretary of State for Social Security* [2001] EWHC Admin 260, Administrative Court, where a similar complaint in relation to Housing Benefit (General) Regulations 1987 reg 7(1)(d) was also rejected.

8   SI 1987 No 1971.

occasion, as a condition of entitlement, to change their landlords or avoid particular landlords. The choice made by the secretary of state was one which he was clearly entitled to adopt, most particularly in the absence of availability of any equally effective alternative measure to curb abuse. After anxious scrutiny I have concluded that I should defer to this decision. I find that there is breach of articles 8 and 14.

Split families

11.12 Respect for family life under article 8 was unsuccessfully invoked in *R v Swale BC ex p Marchant*.[9] The applicant's housing benefit was reduced because his home exceeded the size criteria for a house occupied by him alone. Although his children spent alternate weeks with him after he separated from his partner, she was the one in receipt of child benefit, and was accordingly the parent entitled to include the children in her claim for housing benefit. At first instance the judge rejected an argument that article 8 required the state to provide two homes both large enough to accommodate the children of parents who had separated.

Using benefits to control 'bad' landlords and tenants

11.13 The Labour government housing green paper[10] made various proposals for reducing housing benefit anti-social tenants. The use of benefits in this way may be open to challenge, particularly if sufficient safeguards as to appeal mechanisms are not put in place. Furthermore the withdrawal of housing benefit, almost certainly leading to homelessness, may seem a disproportionate response. It should be noted, however, that applications arguing that the suspension of retirement pensions and invalidity benefit for prisoners were in breach of article 1/1 have been held inadmissible by the Commission.[11] This rejection was, however, based on the argument that the prisoners did not have any ongoing living expenses.

Rent control

11.14 Complaints about rent control are generally voiced by landlords, who argue that limitations on the rent they can obtain for their property is

9 (1998) 32 HLR 26, QBD; 32 HLR 856, CA.
10 *Quality and Choice: a Decent Home for All*, (DETR, 2000).
11 *Joseph Szabjer v UK* App No 27004/95; *Walther Clarke v UK* App No 27011/95; and, *George Carlin v UK* App No 27537/95.

a breach of article 1/1. This is an area where the ECtHR has always acknowledged that states have a wide margin of appreciation. Thus in *Mellacher v Austria*[12] rent controls were found to engage article 1/1 since they controlled the use to which the landlord could put the property. The laws were, however, justified as in the general interest. Laws controlling the use of property 'are especially called for and usual in the field of housing, which in our modern societies is a central concern of social and economic policies.'

11.15 An argument that the Rent Acts (Maximum Fair Rents) Order 1999,[13] which restricted increases in registered rents, was in breach of article 1/1 was rejected by the House of Lords in *R v Secretary of State of the Environment Transport and the Regions ex p Spath Holme*.[14] Lord Bingham said at para 51:

> It is an enduring and intractable problem of social policy that those who need relief cannot always be helped without giving relief to those who do not need it. Housing benefit is means-tested, and the allocation of public resources is a matter for ministers, not courts. The hardship which the Order imposed on landlords was a very relevant consideration, but it was for ministers to judge where the balance between the competing interests of landlords and tenants should be struck. It was not unreasonable to provide that the maximum recoverable rents should be the rents registered. The timing and scope of the Order were matters on which the ministers had to form a judgment, and their judgment cannot be stigmatised as perverse. There was no breach of the European Convention: the European Court of Human Rights has recognised the need for a wide measure of discretion in the implementation of policy in this field, as shown by *Mellacher v Austria* (1989) 12 EHRR 391. Any actions the ministers took, or any failure by the ministers to take action, were bound to be bitterly resented by those who were disadvantaged as a result. That does not mean that the action which the ministers did take in making the Order was unreasonable, unfair or disproportionate, disadvantageous to landlords though it certainly was.

---

12 (1989) 12 EHRR 391, ECtHR.
13 SI No 6. Made under the Landlord and Tenant Act 1985 s31.
14 (2001) 33 HLR 31.

PART III

Practice and procedure

CHAPTER 12

Preliminary issues

How the Human Rights Act 1998 works

12.1   The European Convention of Human Rights and Fundamental Freedoms[1] ('the Convention') is an international agreement entered into by the member states of the Council of Europe in November 1950. Like all treaties, it is not enforceable in domestic law unless specifically applied. The HRA 1998 makes the principal rights and freedoms enshrined in the Convention directly enforceable in domestic courts and tribunals.

Which rights are enforceable?

12.2   The HRA 1998 applies to:

a) articles 2 to 12 and 14 of the Convention;
b) articles 1 to 3 of the First Protocol to the Convention; and
c) articles 1 and 2 of the Sixth Protocol.[2]

These are, in effect, the substantial rights secured by the Convention and are referred to collectively in HRA 1998 as 'the Convention rights'.[3]

How the Convention rights affect domestic law

12.3   In essence, the effect of HRA 1998 is fivefold:

1) to require the government to consider whether proposed legislation is compatible with the Convention rights;
2) to enable the government to amend expeditiously legislation which is incompatible with the Convention rights;
3) to require all legislation to be interpreted and given effect in a way which is compatible with the Convention rights;

---

1   Cmnd 8969.
2   HRA 1998 s1(1); the rights are set out in full in Schedule 1 and must be read with article 16 (restrictions on political activity of aliens), article 17 (prohibition of abuse of rights) and article 18 (limitation on use of restrictions on rights). They are qualified by certain 'derogations and reservations' which limit their application in English law: see HRA 1998 ss14, 15, Sch 3, Human Rights Act (Amendment) Order 2001 SI No 1216.
3   Article 1 requires the contracting states to secure the rights in the Convention to everyone within their jurisdiction and article 13 to provide an effective remedy in the case of a violation. The government's view is that both are given effect to by the HRA 1998 itself.

4) to make it unlawful for a public authority to act in a way which is incompatible with the Convention rights; and

5) to require all courts and tribunals to take into account the Strasbourg jurisprudence when interpreting the Convention rights.

Proposed legislation

12.4 Although there is nothing to prevent Parliament passing legislation which is incompatible with a Convention right, the government of the day must address the issue when promoting Bills. Accordingly, before the second reading in either House, the responsible minister must make a statement[4] either that its provisions are compatible with the Convention rights ('a statement of compatibility') or that, although he or she is unable to make a statement of compatibility, the government nevertheless wishes the House to proceed with the Bill.[5]

Remedial orders

12.5 The HRA 1998 makes provision for a 'fast-track' method to enable incompatible primary and subordinate legislation to be amended by a special order being placed before Parliament.[6]

12.6 The power is conferred in three instances:

a) where a court has declared legislation to be incompatible;[7]

b) where it appears to the government[8] that, having regard to a finding of the European Court of Human Rights which has been made after the HRA 1998 came into force in proceedings against the United Kingdom, a provision of legislation is incompatible with an obligation of the United Kingdom arising from the Convention;[9] and

c) where a provision of subordinate legislation has been quashed or

---

4   It must be in writing and published: HRA 1998 s19(2).

5   HRA 1998 s19(1).

6   HRA 1998 s10, Sch 2.

7   Provided that – where there is a right of appeal – all the parties who could appeal have stated in writing that they do not intend to do so, or no appeal has been brought and it is now out of time for doing so, or any appeal which has been brought has been determined or abandoned: HRA 1998 s10(1)(a).

8   The minister or the Sovereign in Council.

9   HRA 1998 s10(1)(b).

declared invalid because of its incompatibility and the minister proposes to use the urgency procedure.[10]

The minister may only exercise the power to make a remedial order if he or she considers that there are compelling reasons for so doing.[11]

Statutory interpretation

12.7   By HRA 1998 s3(1), all legislation must – so far as it is possible – be read and given effect in a way which is compatible with the Convention rights. This requirement applies whenever it was enacted.[12] It is thus retrospective to the extent that it affects the interpretation of legislation in force before the HRA 1998 came into force.

12.8   In *Poplar Housing and Regeneration Community Association Ltd v Donoghue*[13] the Court of Appeal acknowledged that this provision represents a radical departure from the court's traditional role in relation to interpretation. Thus, the primary task of identifying the intention of Parliament must be adjusted to give effect to the direction contained in HRA 1998 s3. Lord Woolf CJ held:[14]

a) section 3 can be ignored unless the legislation being considered would otherwise be in breach of the Convention (courts should always first ascertain whether there would be any breach of the Convention outside section 3);

b) if the court has to rely on section 3, it should limit the extent of the modified meaning to that necessary to achieve compatibility;

c) section 3 does not entitle the courts to *legislate* (their task continues to be one of *interpretation*, but interpretation in accordance with section 3);

d) the views of the parties and the Crown about whether a 'constructive' interpretation should be adopted cannot modify the task of the court (if section 3 applies, the court must adopt the section 3 approach to interpretation).

12.9   Moreover, courts must adopt a method of statutory interpretation

---

10   HRA 1998 s10(4); the urgency procedure enables the minister to make the order without first laying the draft before both Houses of Parliament for 60 days: see HRA 1998 Sch 2, para 4.

11   HRA 1998 s10(2).

12   HRA 1998 s3(2)(a).

13   [2001] EWCA Civ 595; 3 WLR 183, CA.

14   At paragraph 75.

which does not necessarily look for the true meaning, but rather a possible meaning that prevents the making of a declaration of incompatibility.[15]

12.10   The HRA 1998, for the purposes of interpretation, makes a distinction between primary and subordinate legislation.

Primary legislation

12.11   Primary legislation is principally any Act of Parliament (whether public general, local and personal or private) but includes' Orders in Council which are made in exercise of the Royal Prerogative or which amend an Act and Measures of the Church Assembly and the General Synod of the Church of England.[16]

12.12   Where it is not possible to interpret primary legislation compatibly, the court or tribunal must nevertheless apply it (despite its incompatibility).[17] In such cases, the higher courts may make a declaration of incompatibility, which has no effect on the validity, continuing operation or enforcement of the particular provision it applies to and is not binding on the parties to the proceedings in which it is made (see paras 14.64–14.69, below: declarations of incompatibility).[18]

Subordinate legislation

12.13   Subordinate legislation is defined as Orders in Council (other than those which are primary legislation), orders, rules, regulations, schemes, warrants, byelaws or other instruments made under primary legislation (except to the extent to which they operate to bring a provision of that legislation into force or amend any primary legislation).[19]

12.14   If subordinate legislation is found to be incompatible, the court or tribunal must only apply it if – disregarding any possibility of revocation – primary legislation prevents the removal of the

---

15 *W B C v K* [2001] ACD 41, CA.

16 HRA 1998 s21(1); it also includes an order or other instrument made under primary legislation (otherwise than by the National Assembly for Wales) so far as it brings a provision of that legislation into force or amends any primary legislation.

17 HRA 1998 s3(2)(b).

18 HRA 1998 s4(6).

19 HRA 1998 s21(1).

incompatibility.[20] It follows that subordinate legislation must be ignored if primary legislation does not prevent its removal.

Incompatible actions of public authorities

12.15   The HRA 1998 makes it is unlawful for a public authority to act in way which is incompatible with a Convention right.[21] This is both a 'sword and a shield' in civil proceedings; it gives rise to a new cause of action and may be relied on in any legal proceedings, for instance as a defence.[22]

12.16   Thus the HRA 1998 has a direct impact on the legal relationship between the citizen and public authorities. This 'vertical' effect is, however, accompanied by a 'horizontal effect'. Because courts and tribunals are public authorities (see paras 13.5–13.40, below), they are required to act compatibly with the Convention rights both in the interpretation of legislation[23] and generally.[24] They must, therefore, have regard to Convention rights in any case they deal with, regardless of whether a public authority is one of the parties.

Interpretation of the Convention rights

12.17   When a court or tribunal determines a question that has arisen in connection with a Convention right, it must take into account any judgments, decisions, declarations and advisory opinions of the European Court of Human Rights, opinions and decisions of the European Commission of Human Rights and decisions of the Committee of Ministers.[25] This is a continuing obligation which applies regardless of whether the judgment, decision, etc, was made or given before or after the HRA 1998 came into force.[26]

20   HRA 1998 s3(2)(c).
21   HRA 1998 s6.
22   HRA 1998 s7(1).
23   HRA 1998 s3(1).
24   HRA 1998 s6(1).
25   HRA 1998 s2(1).
26   HRA 1998 s2(1).

CHAPTER 13

Enforcement of Convention rights

Acting in a way which is incompatible with Convention rights

13.1   It is unlawful for a public authority to act in way which is incompatible with a Convention right.[1] It is not, however, unlawful to act (or to fail to act) where – in effect – primary legislation requires the authority to act incompatibly (see the statutory defences at para 13.62, below).[2]

Acts

13.2   An act generally includes a failure to act.[3] There is no reason to limit an act (or a failure to act) to operational or executive matters. The taking of a decision or the refusal to take a decision is clearly capable of being an act for the purposes of the HRA 1998. It follows that, for instance, an authority's decision to adopt a policy for the allocation of housing accommodation is justiciable under the HRA 1998 as well as an actual allocation to an individual made as a result of that policy.

13.3   Although having a legal personality, public authorities can only act through their servants or agents. There is no question of the authority being vicariously liable,[4] because servants or agents cannot generally be liable under HRA 1998 s6(1).[5] It follows that public authorities are only liable where they have expressly or impliedly authorised or adopted the actions of their servants or agents.

Against whom can Convention rights be enforced?

13.4   Convention rights can only be directly enforced, using HRA 1998 s6, against public authorities.

Public authorities

13.5   The HRA 1998 does not define a public authority. Expressly included, however, are courts and tribunals and any person with public

1   HRA 1998 s6(1).
2   HRA 1998 s6(2).
3   HRA 1998 s6(6); the only exceptions are a failure to put legislative proposals before Parliament and to make any primary legislation or remedial order.
4   The doctrine of vicarious liability is based on the theory that the superior is responsible for the unlawful acts of the subordinate.
5   Unless they themselves have functions which are of a public nature: see HRA 1998 s6(3)(b).

functions.[6] Expressly excluded are both Houses of Parliament[7] and persons exercising functions in connection with proceedings in Parliament.[8]

13.6 It follows that – for the purposes of the HRA 1998 – there are three types of public authority:

a) 'obvious' or 'standard' public authorities which are public authorities in respect of everything they do;

b) 'hybrid' or 'functional' public authorities, some of whose functions are public; they are only public authorities in respect of acts that are not private;[9] and

c) courts and tribunals.

Standard public authorities

13.7 The absence of a definition in the HRA 1998 leaves the question of what is a public authority to be answered by the common law. For the purposes of bodies subject to judicial review, it is well-established that a public authority is a person or administrative body entrusted with functions to perform for the benefit of the public and not for private profit or gain.[10]

13.8 The issue should, however, be approached with some caution in the light of the decision in *Parochial Church Council of Aston Cantlow and Wilmcote with Billesley, Warwickshire v Wallbank and another*,[11] in which the Court of Appeal commented that, while relevant, the earlier case-law on judicial review was not necessarily determinative of whether a body was a public authority (either standard or functional) for the purposes of the HRA 1998. Rejecting the proposition that the issue could be resolved solely by considering whether a body performed functions of a public nature, the court held that the claimant

---

6   HRA 1998 s6(3).

7   Other than the Judicial Committee of the House of Lords: HRA 1998 s6(4).

8   HRA 1998 s6(3).

9   The dichotomy between standard and functional authorities reflects the government's view – as expressed in Parliamentary debate during the passage of the Bill (see the Lord Chancellor, *Hansard*, HL, 24 November 1997, col 811, and the Home Secretary, *Hansard*, HC, 17 June 1998, cols 409–410) – and was subsequently approved, albeit without much discussion, by the Court of Appeal in *Poplar Housing and Regeneration Community Association v Donoghue* [2001] EWCA Civ 595; [2001] 3 WLR 183, CA, at para 63.

10 *Attorney-General v Company of Proprietors of Margate Pier and Harbour* [1900] 1 Ch 749, ChD; see also *Welch v Bank of England and others* [1955] Ch 508 at 541, ChD; *Director of Public Prosecutions v Manners* [1978] AC 43, CA.

11 [2001] EWCA Civ 713; (2001) *Times* 15 June.

was a public authority because it was created and empowered by law, it was part of the church established by law and its functions included the enforcement through the courts of a common law liability against persons who need not be members of that church.

13.9   There is no difficulty in saying that both central and local government are standard public authorities; as are – what might loosely be termed – emanations of the state, such as the established church, the police and the armed forces. More precise boundaries will need to be mapped by case-law.

Functional public authorities

13.10   The Human Rights Act 1998 s6(3)(b) provides that a public authority includes 'any person[12] certain of whose functions are functions of a public nature.' This is subject to a limitation that a person is not a public authority if (in relation to a particular act[13]) 'the nature of [that] act is private'.[14] It follows that a functional public authority body is not treated as a public authority in respect of private acts.

Functions of a public nature

13.11   Prior to the HRA 1998 coming into force, it was held that, in order to ascertain the nature of a body's functions, there had to be a public law element in relation to its functions and the source of its powers. These were to be given different weight according to the circumstances of the case; moreover, that element was lacking where the source of a power was solely contractual.[15]

13.12   In the first case on the point under the HRA 1998, *Poplar HARCA Ltd v Donoghue*,[16] the Court of Appeal gave the following guidance for determining whether a body was a functional public authority:

1) The definition of who is a public authority and what is a public function should be given a generous interpretation.[17]

---

12 A 'person' means a legal person, that is any individual or body with a legal personality, such as a company, but not an unincorporated association.

13 Which includes a failure to act: HRA 1998 s6(6).

14 HRA 1998 s6(5).

15 *R v Panel on Takeovers and Mergers ex p Datafin plc* [1987] QB 815, CA; the case concerned a body's amenability to judicial review.

16 See note 9, above.

17 See para 58 of the judgment. See also *R (on the application of Heather and others) v The Leonard Cheshire Foundation* [2001] EWHC Admin 429; (2001) 4 CCLR 211, QBD, in which Stanley Burton J took the view that 'public' was construed in *Donoghue* as 'governmental'.

2) The purpose of HRA 1998 s6(3)(b) is to deal with hybrid bodies which have both public and private functions. It is not to make a body, which does not have responsibilities to the public, a public body merely because it performs acts on behalf of a public body which would constitute public functions were such acts to be performed by the public body itself.[18]

3) The emphasis in HRA 1998 s6 on public functions reflects the approach of the courts and text books since the decision in *Datafin*.[19]

4) The fact that a body performs an activity, which otherwise a public body would be under a duty to perform, does not mean that such performance is necessarily a public function. In particular, the provision of accommodation is not, without more, a public function for the purposes of HRA 1998 s6.[20]

Private acts

13.13   The court in *Donoghue* also addressed the circumstances in which the nature of an act is private, in particular:

1) An act can remain of a private nature even though it is performed because another body is under a public duty to ensure that that act is performed.[21]

2) What can make an act – which would otherwise be private – public, is a feature or a combination of features which impose a public character or stamp on the act.[22]

3) The following are indicators of an act having a public character:
   (a) there is statutory authority for what is done;
   (b) the extent of control over the function exercised by another body which is a public authority; and
   (c) the proximity of the act to the activities of the public body (in other words, the more closely the act that could be of a private nature is enmeshed in the activities of a public body, the more likely it is to be public).[23]

---

18 Ibid para 59.

19 Ibid para 65; see also *Parochial Church Council of Aston Cantlow and Wilmcote with Billesley, Warwickshire v Wallbank and another* [2001] EWCA Civ 713; (2001) *Times* 15 June, in which the Court of Appeal acknowledged the importance of a function-based approach to the hybrid class of public authority.

20 *Poplar HARCA Ltd v Donoghue* [2001] EWCA Civ 595; [2001] 3 WLR 183, CA, para 65.

21 Ibid para 59.

22 Ibid para 65.

23 Ibid para 65.

4) The fact that acts are supervised by a public regulatory body does not necessarily indicate that they are of a public nature.[24]

Who are public authorities in relation to housing?

The Crown

13.14   The Crown[25] is a large landowner, whose estate includes residential property. Crown property[26] may be managed by the Crown Estate Commissioners or a government department.

13.15   The Crown is a standard public authority for the purposes of the HRA 1998.

Local authorities

13.16   Local authorities (whether exercising housing or social services functions) are undoubtedly standard public authorities.

13.17   As such, they are public authorities for all purposes, this includes not just the functions they are statutorily obliged to perform for the benefit of the public at large – for instance, public health, housing the homeless and allocating housing accommodation – but also the provision of accommodation, including the obligation to repair stemming from a contractual agreement and the right to recover possession.

'Quasi' local authorities

13.18   Falling under this somewhat inelegant heading is a variety of statutory bodies, all of whom are likely to be standard public authorities, principally because they exercise public functions and have a statutory basis for their existence.

13.19   The most important of these are housing action trusts ('HATs')[27] A HAT is a statutory corporation[28] to which local authority housing stock is transferred. Its primary objects include the repair or improvement of that stock, the securing or facilitating of the improvement of living and social conditions in the area and its general environment, the encouragement of diversity in the interests by virtue of which

---

24   Ibid para 65; by analogy to the position in judicial review, where a regulatory body may be deemed public but the activities of the body which is regulated may be categorised as private.

25   The Crown is expressly bound: HRA 1998 s22(5).

26   Which may be an interest in the Crown Estate or one belonging to the Queen, the Chancellor of the Duchy of Lancaster, the Duchy of Cornwall or a government department.

27   See Housing Act 1988 (HA 1988) Pt III.

28   HA 1988 s62 and Sch 7.

housing accommodation in the area is occupied and, in the case of accommodation which is occupied under tenancies, diversity in the identity of the landlords.[29]

13.20 Others include urban development corporations,[30] new town corporations,[31] the Development Board for Rural Wales,[32] waste disposal authorities[33] and residuary bodies,[34] all of which have housing functions to a greater or lesser degree.

Registered social landlords

13.21 Registered social landlords ('RSLs') are the following bodies that are registered with the Housing Corporation:[35]

a) housing associations (see para 13.27, below) that are registered charities;[36]

b) housing associations that are industrial and provident societies;[37] and

c) housing companies.[38]

However, industrial and provident societies and companies must be non-profit-making and carry out designated housing-related activities.[39]

13.22 Registered social landlords – in effect – bridge the gap between the public and the private sector and exhibit features common to both.[40] Thus the requirement to register with the Housing Corporation (which acts as a regulator of their activities), the receipt of public funds and the statutory control of the allocation of assured tenancies in respect of local authority nominations[41] all point to the public nature of their functions. Conversely, different characteristics

---

29 HA 1988 s63.
30 An earlier incarnation of a HAT, with similar purposes: see Local Government, Planning and Land Act 1980 Pt XVI.
31 For instance, a new town development corporation (see New Towns Act 1981) or the Commission for New Towns.
32 See Development of Rural Wales Act 1976.
33 See Local Government Act 1985 (LGA 1985).
34 See LGA 1985.
35 Housing Act 1996 (HA 1996) ss1 and 56.
36 Registered under the Charities Act 1993 s3.
37 Registered under the Industrial and Provident Societies Act 1965 s1.
38 Incorporated (with or without limited liability) under the Companies Act 1985 s1.
39 HA 1996 s2(1), (2).
40 For instance, the provision of housing out of public funds.
41 Under HA 1996 s159(2).

suggest otherwise, for instance, their structure is that of a private law entity, members of the board are usually private individuals not answerable to government and they rely (to a substantial degree) on private finance.[42]

13.23   The English courts[43] have refused to treat housing associations as public authorities in relation to either landlord and tenant disputes[44] or the management of a residential home for the performance of a local housing authority's statutory duties.[45] Both of these cases, however, were decided before the HRA 1998 came into force in relation to amenability to judicial review, when the issue was whether the organisation as a whole was a public body, rather then whether its individual functions were public in nature.

13.24   It was held in *Donoghue* that, for the purposes of the HRA 1998, although RSLs (as a class) are not standard public authorities, they are nevertheless capable of being functional authorities.[46] Whether an individual RSL is or is not a public authority requires a detailed examination of its functions, and why and how it carries them out. Even if it is, it is still necessary to ask whether the act in question is private. In the final analysis it is a question of fact and degree.

13.25   In *Donoghue*, the claimant landlord was a bespoke housing association created by a local authority for the purpose of taking a transfer of that authority's housing stock. Five of its members were also members of the local authority and it was subject to local authority guidance as to how it acted towards its tenants; at the time of the transfer of the housing stock, the defendant was a tenant of the local authority and it was intended that – on being transferred – she would be in no better or worse position than if she had remained the tenant of the local authority. The court held that the defendant's landlord was a functional public authority because – taking into account all the circumstances – the role of the housing association was so closely assimilated to that of the local authority that it was performing public

---

42 Even those in receipt of public funds have to raise a substantial proportion of their running costs privately (ie, through rents and loans from private financial institutions).

43 In Scotland, a housing association has been held to be a public authority when exercising statutory powers: *Boyle v Castlemilk East Housing Co-operative Ltd* (1997) *Times* 16 May.

44 *Peabody Housing Association v Greene* (1978) 38 P & CR 644, CA.

45 *R v Servite Houses and Wandsworth LBC ex p Goldsmith and Chatting*, (2000) 3 CCLR 325; (2000) 32 HLR 35, QBD.

46 *Poplar HARCA Ltd v Donoghue* [2001] EWCA Civ 595; [2001] 3 WLR 183, CA, at para 63.

and not private functions and that the act of providing accommodation for the tenant was not private.[47]

13.26   Given the variety of RSLs, it is necessary to consider both whether a particular RSL exercises public functions and whether the act complained of is public on the facts of the individual case.

Unregistered housing associations

13.27   A housing association is a society, body of trustees or company, which is established for the purpose of, or amongst whose objects or powers are included those of, providing, constructing, improving or managing, or facilitating or encouraging the construction or improvement of, housing accommodation, and which does not trade for profit or whose constitution or rules prohibit the issue of capital with interest or dividend exceeding a prescribed rate.[48]

13.28   Not all housing associations are registered with the Housing Corporation, in particular, associations discharging local authority duties, fully mutual co-operative housing associations, charitable housing trusts, self-build housing societies and industrial housing associations.

13.29   An unregistered housing association which enters into an agreement (approved by the Secretary of State) for the purpose of discharging local authority duties may be a functional public authority.[49] In each case, it is necessary to examine the circumstances to see if the necessary public element is present.

13.30   Fully mutual co-operative housing associations are associations which restrict membership to tenants or prospective tenants and which are registered as industrial and provident societies.[50] The lack of a public element and the high degree of mutuality[51] indicate that they are very unlikely to be public authorities for the purposes of the HRA 1998.

13.31   Charitable housing trusts[52] which are not registered with the Housing Corporation enjoy special statutory treatment to the extent

---

47 Ibid at para 66.
48 HA 1985 s5 and the Housing Association Act 1985 (HAA 1985) s1.
49 Pursuant to HA 1995 s27.
50 HA 1985 s5(2), HAA 1985 s1(2).
51 In *Parochial Church Council of Aston Cantlow and Wilmcote with Billesley, Warwickshire v Wallbank and another* [2001] EWCA Civ 713; (2001) *Times* 15 June, CA, the court drew a conceptual line between functions of public governance and functions of mutual governance (see also *R v Disciplinary Committee of the Jockey Club ex p Aga Khan* [1993] 1 WLR 909, CA).
52 As defined by HA 1985 s6, HAA 1985 s2.

that they may transfer their housing to local authorities[53] and the Secretary of State may certify the Attorney-General to institute or intervene in legal proceedings in respect of their property.[54] It is the authors' view that this is unlikely to be sufficient to make them functional public authorities.

13.32   Self-build housing societies are housing associations whose objects are to provide dwellings for sale to, or occupation by, their members. Dwellings are built or improved principally with the use of their members' own labour.[55] They are eligible to receive loans from the Housing Corporation and enjoy tax privileges. This is insufficient to make them public authorities.

13.33   Industrial housing associations are housing associations established by employers for the benefit of their employees. The high degree of mutuality[56] makes it highly unlikely that they will be treated as public authorities.

Others

13.34   The following bodies, which are established for the public benefit, are likely to be standard public authorities: National Health Service trusts,[57] the Church of England,[58] police and fire authorities, the Housing Corporation[59], the Commissioner for Local Government ('the Local Government Ombudsman'), and the Housing Ombudsman.[60]

13.35   Housing co-operatives (commonly called 'management co-operatives') are co-operatives formed, with the consent of the Secretary of State, to take over the whole or part of a local authority's management responsibilities.[61] If entered into before the commencement of the Housing and Planning Act 1986, such agreements can include the power to let land. Tenants of co-operatives are secure tenants.

---

53 HAA 1985 s35.

54 HAA 1985 s36.

55 HAA 1985 s1(3).

56 See *Parochial Church Council of Aston Cantlow and Wilmcote with Billesley, Warwickshire v Wallbank and another*, at note 51, above.

57 In particular, National Health Service and Community Care Act 1990 Sch 8 para 19 which excludes protection for certain tenants whose landlord is an NHS trust which is deemed to be a government department for this purpose.

58 *Parochial Church Council of Aston Cantlow and Wilmcote with Billesley, Warwickshire v Wallbank and another*, at note 51, above.

59 See HAA 1985 Pt III.

60 Established pursuant to HA 1996 s51, Sch 2.

61 See HA 1985 s27.

Housing co-operatives may be capable of being functional public authorities, if the necessary public element is present.

Private landlords

13.36   Private landlords frequently do things by arrangement with public authorities, such as providing temporary accommodation to the homeless. It is clear that – by doing so – they cannot be said to be carrying out public functions, because the mere execution of an action on behalf of a public authority, whether by informal or contractual arrangement does not amount to the performance of a function.[62]

Courts and tribunals

13.37   The HRA 1998 expressly provides for courts and tribunals to be public authorities.[63] As a 'court' is not defined, it must be given its ordinary meaning. In *Halsbury's Laws*[64] a court is said to mean both a 'place where justice is administered' and 'the persons who exercise judicial functions under authority derived directly or indirectly from the Sovereign'.[65] In terms of housing, all courts in which housing cases are heard are public authorities, ranging from county and magistrates' courts to the House of Lords.

13.38   The position of tribunals is less clear. A tribunal is sometimes used as an alternative to or as a generic term for courts, judges and formal decision-making bodies. In the HRA 1998, a tribunal is defined as 'any tribunal in which legal proceedings may be brought.'[66] No indication is given, however, as to what is meant by 'legal proceedings'. It is suggested that the term requires the adjudication of a legal issue and must be contrasted with proceedings which are merely administrative.

13.39   With this in mind, there is no difficulty in saying that rent assessment committees, housing benefit appeal tribunals,[67] leasehold valuation tribunals and the Lands Tribunal are tribunals for the purposes of the HRA 1998.

---

62   *Poplar HARCA Ltd v Donoghue* [2001] EWCA Civ 595; [2001] 3 WLR 183, CA, at para 65.
63   HRA 1998 s6(3).
64   4th edition (Butterworths).
65   See para 701.
66   HRA 1998 s21(1).
67   Who, from 2 July 2001, assumed the functions of housing benefit review boards: see Housing Benefit and Council Tax Benefit (Decisions and Appeals) Regulations 2001 SI No 1002.

13.40   On the other hand, rent officers, agricultural dwelling-house advisory committees[70] and housing benefit review officers,[71] are not because their functions are administrative. For the same reason, bodies established by public authorities to conduct internal reviews or appeals are not tribunals. This is so whether there is a statutory requirement to do so, such as in relation to homelessness[72] and the allocation of housing accommodation,[73] or whether the exercise is purely voluntary, for example, to review a decision to evict a tenant. In any event, the issue is somewhat academic if the administrative tribunal is established by a standard public authority.[74]

Raising Convention rights in legal proceedings

13.41   Convention rights may be enforced in one of two ways. A claim may be brought in a court[75] against a public authority for acting incompatibly with a Convention right ('a human rights claim'). Alternatively, reliance may be placed on a Convention right in any legal proceedings before a court or tribunal ('reliance on human rights'). In either case, however, the person relying on the Convention right must be a victim of the allegedly unlawful action (see paras 13.52–13.61 below).[76]

13.42   In accordance with its legislative purpose of creating a floor of rights,[77] the HRA 1998 expressly provides that reliance on a Convention right does not restrict any other right or freedom enjoyed under United Kingdom law; nor does it restrict a person's right to make any claim or bring any proceedings which he or she could make or bring other than under the HRA 1998.[78] A human rights claim may thus stand alone or run in parallel with any other claim.

---

70 Established for the purposes of advising whether a local authority should provide suitable alternative accommodation in the interests of efficient agriculture: see Rent (Agriculture) Act 1976 Pt IV.

71 Housing Benefit (General) Regulations 1987 SI No 1971 reg 79(2).

72 HA 1996 s202(4).

73 HA 1996 s164(5).

74 HRA 1998 s6(3)(b).

75 But not a tribunal.

76 HRA 1998 s7(1).

77 Lord Chancellor, *Hansard* HL, 18 November 1997, col 510.

78 HRA 1998 s11.

Bringing a human rights claim

13.43 A human rights claim[79] may only be made in respect of an act taking place on or after 2 October 2000.[80]

13.44 A claim may be brought in an appropriate court or tribunal, which means a court or tribunal as determined by rules.[81] To date, no tribunals have been given jurisdiction to hear human rights claims[82] (and the government has no present intention of doing so), but the Civil Procedure Rules 1998[83] ('the CPR') provide for claims to be brought in the High Court or a county court.

13.45 Claims may be brought either:

a) against a public authority which has acted or proposes to act incompatibly with a Convention right; or

b) in respect of judicial acts.

Claims that a public authority has acted unlawfully

13.46 Proceedings against a public authority under HRA 1998 s7 can only be brought in one of three ways:

1) In a county court or in the High Court alleging incompatible action by a public authority; for instance, that a local housing authority had violated article 1/1 (protection of property) by evicting a tenant.

2) In a county court or in the High Court following a finding by another court or tribunal that a public authority had acted incompatibly under HRA 1998 s7(1)(b), where that other court or tribunal lacked the power to grant the relief or remedy available in the county court or the High Court; for instance, a claim for damages founded on a finding by a magistrates' court that a local authority had acted incompatibly with a Convention right in relation to the service of an abatement notice.[84]

3) In the High Court for judicial review; for example a claim that a local housing authority's decision on an application for a transfer is incompatible with article 8 (the right to respect for private and family life).

79 Which includes a counterclaim or a similar proceeding: HRA 1998 s7(2).
80 For instance, the date HRA 1998 s7 came into force: HRA 1998 s22(4).
81 HRA 1998 s7(1)(a), (2); 'the rules' means rules made by the Lord Chancellor or the Secretary of State for the purposes of this section or rules of court.
82 HRA 1998 s7(2).
83 See Civil Procedure (Amendment No 4) Rules 2000 SI No 2092.
84 Under Environmental Protection Act (EPA) 1990 s80.

Proceedings in respect of judicial acts

13.47   Where the claimant claims in respect of a judicial act, proceedings may only be brought in one of three ways:[85]

a) by exercising a right of appeal,[86]
b) on an application for judicial review,[87] or
c) as a claim in the High Court.[88]

Judicial acts

13.48   A 'judicial act' means a judicial act of a court or tribunal and includes an act done on the instructions, or on behalf, of a judge.[89] There is no definition of a 'judge' in the HRA 1998; its ordinary meaning is 'one invested with authority to determine any cause or question in a court of judicature.'[90] The term clearly applies to a district judge, a circuit judge, a High Court judge (and a deputy), a Lord Justice of Appeal and a Lord of Appeal in Ordinary. In addition, HRA 1998 expressly includes – for the purposes of proceedings brought in respect of a judicial act – a member of a tribunal, a justice of the peace and a clerk or other officer entitled to exercise the jurisdiction of a court or a tribunal.[91]

13.49   Unless done under judicial direction or on behalf of a member of the judiciary, therefore, acts of the administrative staff are not judicial acts. Thus the arrest of a person by a bailiff on the order of a judge is a judicial act, but the refusal of a county court officer to accept an application to suspend a warrant for possession is not. Courts and tribunals are, however, public authorities,[92] and so such an act would be actionable as a failure to act compatibly under HRA 1998 s7(1).

---

85   HRA 1998 s9(1).
86   If the claim is made in an appellant's notice, it will be dealt with according to the normal rules governing where that appeal is heard: CPR PD 7 para 6.5(2).
87   This does not affect any rule of law which prevents a court from being the subject of judicial review: HRA 1998 s9(2).
88   HRA 1998 s9(1)(c); CPR 7.11.
89   HRA 1998 s9(5).
90   See *Jowitt's Dictionary of English Law* (Sweet & Maxwell).
91   HRA 1998 s9(5).
92   HRA 1998 s6(3).

Reliance on human rights

13.50   A person who claims that a public authority has acted (or proposes to act) incompatibly with a Convention right may rely on that Convention right in any legal proceedings[93] (see para 14.12, below).

13.51   Unlike where a claim is brought against a public authority, the entitlement to rely on Convention rights applies whenever the allegedly unlawful act took place, ie, including acts which occurred before the HRA 1998 came into force.[94]

Who can enforce Convention rights?

Victims

13.52   Only a 'victim'[95] of an unlawful act may bring a human rights claim or rely on human rights in legal proceedings.[96]

Generally

13.53   A person is a victim of an unlawful act only if he would be a victim for the purposes of article 34 of the Convention (see paras 13.55–13.61, below) were proceedings to be brought in the European Court of Human Rights (ECtHR) in respect of that act.[97]

In judicial review proceedings

13.54   In general, a person seeking judicial review must have 'sufficient interest' in the matter to which the claim relates.[98] What amounts to sufficient interest is a question of mixed fact and law. The HRA 1998 overlays this with a further requirement for the claimant to be a victim (or potential victim) of that act.[99] In practice, this is likely to make little difference to the vast majority of judicial review cases in which the claimant is clearly directly affected by the act or omission of the public authority. In exceptional cases, public interest groups –

93 HRA 1998 7(1)(b).
94 HRA 1998 s22(4).
95 Or a person who would be a victim in the case of a proposed unlawful act: HRA 1998 s7(1)(b).
96 HRA 1998 s7(1).
97 HRA 1998 s7(7).
98 Supreme Court Act 1981 s31(3); CPR Pt 54.
99 HRA 1998 s7(3).

although generally having standing to apply for judicial review[100] – will not be able to rely on human rights grounds because they would fail the victim test.

Article 34 of the Convention

13.55   The relevant part of Article 34 provides that the ECtHR:

> ... may receive applications from any person, non-governmental organisation or group of individuals claiming to be the victim of a violation by one of the High Contracting Parties of the rights set forth in the Convention or the protocols thereto ...

Breadth of meaning

13.56   Self-evidently there is no definition of victim within article 34 and its meaning is therefore derived from Strasbourg case-law. The categories are widely drawn and have been held to include companies,[101] trade unions,[102] churches,[103] professional associations[104] and political parties,[105] although there are clearly some rights – such as the right to life (article 2) and the right to respect for private and family life (article 8) – which by their very nature preclude non-natural persons from being victims. Public authorities themselves, such as local government institutions or semi-state bodies cannot be victims.[106]

Must be in the jurisdiction

13.57   A particular legal status, such as citizenship or residence, is not a pre-requisite. It is actual presence within the jurisdiction that must be established.[107] In this regard, whether a person is a victim is a ques-

---

100   See, for instance, *R v Secretary of State for Social Services ex p CPAG* (1984) *Times* 16 August. In *R v HM Inspectorate of Pollution and the Ministry of Agriculture, Fisheries and Food ex p Greenpeace Ltd* [1994] COD 116, it was held that the question of standing is a matter for the discretion of the court.

101   *Pine Valley Developments Ltd v Ireland* (1991) Series A No 222, 14 EHRR 319, ECtHR, at para 40–43; *Autronic AG v Switzerland* (1990) Series A No 178, (1990) 12 EHRR 485, ECtHR.

102   *CCSU v United Kingdom* (1987) 50 DR 228, 10 EHRR 269, ECtHR.

103   *Church of Scientology v Sweden* (1980) 21 DR 109.

104   *Asociación de Aviadores de la Republica v Spain* (1988) 41 DR 211.

105   *United Communist Party of Turkey v Turkey* (1998) 26 EHRR 121, ECtHR; *Liberal Party v United Kingdom* (1980) 21 DR 211, 4 EHRR 106, ECtHR.

106   *Rothenthurm Commune v Switzerland* (1988) 59 DR 251; *Ayuntamiento de M v Spain* (1991) 68 DR 209.

107   This is clear from the words of article 1: 'The High Contracting Parties shall secure to everyone within their jurisdiction the rights and freedoms defined in section 1 of the Convention.'

tion of fact rather than law.[108] Thus a person who had illegally entered the United Kingdom can be a victim, whereas a British citizen physically outside the jurisdiction cannot. So, for instance, an illegal immigrant would be a victim in respect of a local authority's decision that he or she could not apply for homelessness assistance under HA 1996 Pt VII.

Must be directly affected

13.58 In general, only a person directly affected (or likely to be directly affected) by an act or omission can be a victim.[109] Hypothetical breaches are not actionable nor may public interest litigation be instituted without a victim.[110] This requirement is mitigated to some degree to enable a person who is indirectly affected to complain where the person directly affected is unable[111] or unwilling to do so.[112]

13.59 It is possible to be directly affected without suffering any detriment; it is enough that there is a risk of being directly affected.[113] The degree of risk often turns on the facts of the individual case and the

---

108 See *Bertrand Russell Peace Foundation Ltd v United Kingdom* (1978) 14 DR 117, where residence (without actual presence) was held to be insufficient.

109 *Amuur v France* (1996) 22 EHRR 533, ECtHR.

110 But see the approach adopted in covert surveillance cases where the very secrecy underpinning the complaint often makes it difficult to show direct effect: *Klass v Federal Republic of Germany* (1978) Series A No 28, 2 EHRR 214, ECtHR; *Hilton v United Kingdom* (1988) 57 DR 108.

111 See *Wolgram v Federal Republic of Germany* (1986) 46 DR 213, 9 EHRR 548, ECtHR, *Sadik v Greece* (1997) 24 EHRR 321 (relatives of persons directly affected who had died); *Abdulaziz, Cabales and Balkandali v United Kingdom* (1985) Series A No 94, 7 EHRR 471, ECtHR (relatives of persons who had been refused permission to enter the UK).

112 See *Paton v United Kingdom* (1980) 19 DR 244, 3 EHRR 408, ECtHR (a prospective father was a victim for the purposes of a right to life claim (article 2) in respect of the termination of his wife's pregnancy), but compare with *Brüggemann and Sceuten v Germany* (1976) 5 DR 103, (not enough for a man – otherwise unaffected – to maintain that it was his public duty to challenge abortion legislation).

113 There are a number of examples of this approach: *Campbell and Cosans v United Kingdom* (1982) Series A No 48, 4 EHRR 293, ECtHR (risk of corporal punishment at a school); *Marckx v Belgium* (1979) Series A No 31, 4 EHRR 149, ECtHR; *Dudgeon v United Kingdom* (1981) Series A No 45, 4 EHRR 149, ECtHR; *Johnston v Ireland* (1986) Series A No 112, 9 EHRR 203; *Norris v Ireland* (1988) Series A No 142, 13 EHRR 186, ECtHR (membership of a class of persons likely to be adversely affected by legislation); *Open Door Counselling and Dublin Well Woman Centre Ltd v Ireland* (1992) Series A No 246, 15 EHRR 244, ECtHR (risk of being affected by an injunction preventing dissemination of information on abortion).

article allegedly violated, for instance, the possibility of irreparable harm may be enough.[114]

Loss of victim status

13.60 As detriment is not a prerequisite of being a victim, its removal by the state does not necessarily result in that person ceasing to be a victim.[115] An acknowledgement of the substantial violation together with redress, however, has been held to be sufficient for the loss of victim status;[116] similarly, where – even without recognition of the violation – legislation was passed which improved the legal position of the complainant.[117]

Representative actions

13.61 A representative action can be brought on behalf of a victim who lacks capacity, for instance a child or an adult with a learning disability. Where the claimant does not have legal responsibility for the victim, it is necessary to have authority to be the representative.[118] Likewise, unincorporated associations can take action on behalf of members, but only if those members have been directly affected by the act or omission complained of.

The statutory defences

13.62 It is not unlawful for a public authority to act in a way which is incompatible with a Convention right in either of the following circumstances:

a) where, as the result of primary legislation,[119] the authority could not have acted differently;[120] and

b) where the authority was acting so as to give effect to or enforce a provision of, or made under, primary legislation which cannot be

---

114 *Soering v United Kingdom* (1989) Series A No 161, 11 EHRR 439, ECtHR (prospect of a prolonged period on death row).

115 *Eckle v Federal Republic of Germany* (1982) Series A No 51, 5 EHRR 1, ECtHR; *Lüdi v Switzerland* (1992) Series A No 238, 15 EHRR 173, ECtHR; in Strasbourg jurisprudence, detriment goes to 'just satisfaction', ie, compensation.

116 *Lüdi v Switzerland* at note 115 above.

117 *X v Denmark* (1978) 15 DR 128.

118 *X v Sweden* (1979) 16 DR 105.

119 For which see above, para 12.11.

120 HRA 1998 s6(2)(a).

read or given effect in a way which is compatible with the Convention rights.[121]

13.63 It should, of course, be noted that despite there being such a defence, a court empowered to do so[122] can nevertheless make a declaration of incompatibility in respect of the applicable legislation which does not affect the outcome of the proceedings so far as it concerns the parties to it (see paras 14.64–14.69, below).[123]

Acting in accordance with primary legislation

13.64 Put simply, authorities have a defence if they had no option but to act as they did either because of a requirement of primary legislation or because primary legislation could not be read compatibly.[124] For instance, HA 1996 s202(4) provides for a local housing authority to review its determination of the duty owed to a person applying to it as homeless.[125] A claim that the authority acted in breach of article 6 of the Convention because the review was not independent and impartial could be resisted because primary legislation required the authority to act as it did.

When subordinate legislation may be disregarded

13.65 As with primary legislation, subordinate legislation must, so far as is possible, be read and given effect to in a way which is compatible with Convention rights.[126] If, however, this cannot be done, it must – except in one instance – be ignored or disapplied. The exception is where primary legislation prevents this.

121 HRA 1998 s6(2)(b).
122 See below, para 14.68.
123 HRA 1998 s4(6).
124 Applying the HRA 1998 approach to statutory interpretation under s3 (see paras 12.7–12.9 above).
125 Under HA 1996 Pt VII.
126 HRA 1998 s3(1).

CHAPTER 14

Court and tribunal proceedings

continued

Introduction

14.1 This chapter addresses the practicalities of raising a human rights issue in civil proceedings[1] before English[2] courts[3] and tribunals. The majority of housing cases are litigated in the civil courts and although human rights relating to housing can arise in criminal proceedings (for instance, relating to the abatement of statutory nuisances under EPA 1990 Pt III), such proceedings are outside the scope of this book.[4]

14.2 Except where indicated (see tribunal proceedings at paras 14.70– 14.77, below), the following paragraphs only apply to court proceedings.

14.3 When drafting the HRA 1998, the government's intention was – so far as possible – to keep novel procedures and remedies to a minimum. As a result, the rights created by the HRA 1998 are designed to fit into the existing rules of practice and procedure. It was, however, necessary to make some amendments and additions to the CPR and accompanying practice directions. In general, these changes are limited to:

1) The procedures for dealing with claims brought under the HRA 1998 alone rather than in existing proceedings.
2) Notifying the Crown where the court is considering making a declaration of incompatibility.
3) Joining the Crown to proceedings involving claims for damages in respect of a judicial act.
4) Ensuring that such proceedings are heard in the appropriate court and by the correct judge.
5) The citation of Strasbourg authorities in proceedings.

---

1 Other than in family matters which may have housing implications, for instance, in relation to occupation orders under the Family Law Act 1996 Pt IV. There are supplementary rules; see Family Proceedings (Amendment) Rules 2000 SI No 2267.

2 The HRA 1998 applies to the whole of the United Kingdom; references to Scotland and Northern Ireland have therefore been excluded.

3 For instance, county courts, the High Court and the Court of Appeal but not including proceedings before the Judicial Committee of the House of Lords or the Privy Council, when sitting as civil courts of appeal.

4 Practitioners should be aware that the introduction of the HRA 1998 has necessitated changes to the Criminal Appeal Rules 1968 for criminal proceedings up to and including the Court of Appeal: see Criminal Appeal (Amendment) Rules 2000 SI No 2036.

14.4   Whether pursuing or defending a claim, therefore, practitioners should use existing procedures, subject to the modifications set out below.

14.5   It should be noted that any reference to a claim in proceedings includes a counterclaim or a similar proceeding.[5]

Time limits

Bringing a human rights claim

14.6   As a general rule, a human rights claim must be brought within one year of the date on which the act complained of took place.[6] This may, however, be subject to any shorter time limit which applies to a particular procedure,[7] for instance, if it is raised by way of judicial review, proceedings must be started promptly and in any event within three months of when the ground first arose.[8]

14.7   The court has a discretion to extend time if it considers that it is equitable to do so having regard to all the circumstances.[9]

Reliance on human rights

14.8   The statutory one-year time limit only applies to bringing a human rights claim and not to other proceedings in which reliance is placed on human rights, where the limitation period is that appropriate to the particular cause of action. It should be noted, moreover, that the HRA 1998 does not give the court a power to extend time in such a case.[10]

Raising a human rights issue

Bringing a human rights claim

14.9   A human rights claim[11] may be brought in the High Court or a county

---

5   HRA 1998 s7(2).
6   HRA 1998 s7(5)(a).
7   HRA 1998 s7(5).
8   CPR 54.5(1).
9   HRA 1998 s7(5)(b).
10 See ibid. Any application to extend time, therefore, must be made on the basis applicable to that cause of action.
11 For instance, that a public authority has acted (or proposes to act) incompatibly with a Convention right, contrary to HRA 1998 s6(1).

court,[12] except where it is in respect of a judicial act in which case it must be started in the High Court.[13]

14.10   The normal rules apply when deciding in which court and specialist list a human rights claim should be commenced. They also apply in deciding which procedure to use to start the claim, for instance, CPR Part 7 (claims), Part 8 (alternative procedure) or Part 54 (judicial review).[14]

Reliance on human rights

14.11   Reliance may be placed on human rights 'in any legal proceedings.'[15] It is important not to underestimate this phrase. It remains open to question whether it will blur the procedural divisions between judicial review proceedings and an ordinary action.[16] For instance, it is settled (pre-HRA 1998) law that any challenge to a decision to evict an introductory tenant can only be made by way of judicial review.[17] It is for the courts to decide whether a challenge to such a decision on human rights grounds would be justiciable in the county court, because human rights can be relied on in any legal proceedings.[18]

14.12   'Legal proceedings' include proceedings brought by or at the instigation of a public authority and an appeal against the decision of a court or tribunal.[19]

14.13   Where the first instance hearing of proceedings brought by a public authority took place before the HRA 1998 came into force an appeal by the defendant is part of the 'proceedings'.[20]

---

12   CPR 7.11(2).
13   HRA 1998 s7(2); CPR 7.11(1); CPR PD 7A para 2.10(2).
14   CPR PD 7A para 2.10(1).
15   HRA 1998 s7(1)(b).
16   Well-established since *Cocks v Thanet DC* [1983] 2 AC 286, 6 HLR 15, HL.
17   *Manchester CC v Cochrane* (1999) 31 HLR 810, CA.
18   Note the emphasis put on this phrase by Lord Woolf CJ in *Poplar Housing and Regeneration Community Association Ltd v Donoghue* [2001] EWCA Civ 595; [2001] 3 WLR 183, CA at para 27.
19   HRA 1998 s7(6).
20   *R v Benjafield, R v Leal, R v Rezvi, R v Milford* [2001] 3 WLR 75, CA (a conjoined appeal); see also *R v Director of Public Prosecutions ex p Khebeline and others* [2001] AC 326, HL *per* Lord Steyn at 367H–368C.

Appeals

14.14   An appellate court would appear to have jurisdiction to deal with a human rights point even though it was not raised at first instance.[21] This follows from the court's requirement to act compatibly with Convention rights.[22] Nevertheless, the alleged failure of a lower court to act compatibly with Convention rights cannot be relied on as a ground of appeal where that alleged failure occurred before the HRA 1998 came into force, ie, 2 October 2000.[22a]

14.15   If a human rights claim is made in an appellant's notice, it is dealt with according to the normal rules governing where that appeal is to be heard.[23] For these purposes, a statutory appeal[24] to a county court is an appeal[25].

Statements of case

Generally

14.16   A party to proceedings seeking to rely in a claim on any provision of, or right arising under, the HRA 1998, or seeking a remedy available under it, is required to state that fact in his or her statement of case,[26] which must give precise details of the Convention right that is alleged to have been infringed and details of the infringement.[27] In judicial review proceedings, the same information must be included on the claim form.[28]

14.17   Where reliance is placed on a finding of unlawfulness by another court or tribunal, details of the finding must be provided.[29]

14.18   Where the party relies on a judicial act, which is allegedly in violation of a Convention right, that act and the court or tribunal that is alleged to have made it must be specified.[30]

---

21 See CPR PD 52 para 5.1A which clearly contemplates this occurrence.

22 HRA 1998 s6(1).

22a *Wilson v First County Trust Ltd (No 2)* [2001] EWCA Civ 633; [2001] 3 WLR 42, CA; see also *R v Lambert* [2001] UKHL 37; [2001] 3 WLR 206.

23 CPR PD 7A para 2.10(2).

24 For instance, in relation to homelessness (under HA 1996 Pt VII) or against a demolition order (under HA 1985 Pt IX).

25 *Azimi v Newham LBC* (2001) 33 HLR 51, CA.

26 CPR PD 16 para 16.1(1).

27 CPR PD 16 para 16.1(2)(a).

28 CPR PD 54 para 5.3.

29 CPR PD 16 para 16.1(2)(e).

30 CPR PD 16 para 16.1(2)(f).

Relief and remedies

14.19   The relief sought from the court, for example, damages, must be specified and, if it includes either a declaration of incompatibility (see paras 14.64–14.69, below) or damages in respect of a judicial act (see paras 14.40–14.42, below), the statement of case must include a statement to this effect.[31]

14.20   Where a declaration of incompatibility is sought, precise details of the legislative provision alleged to be incompatible and details of the alleged incompatibility must be given.[32]

14.21   Any claim for damages in respect of a judicial act must be specifically set out.[33]

Amendments

14.22   A party who wishes to amend[34] his or her statement of case in order to rely on the HRA 1998 or to seek a remedy under it must do so as soon as possible, unless the court orders otherwise.[35]

Appeals

14.23   Where – for the first time in an appeal – an appellant wishes to rely on the HRA 1998, or to seek a remedy under it, he or she must include in the appellant's notice the same information as is required in a statement of case in respect of a claim;[36] likewise the same provisions apply in respect of a respondent to an appeal and a respondent's notice.[37] The rules about amending a statement of case apply equally to amending appellant's and respondent's notices.[38]

14.24   Where proceedings in respect of a judicial act are brought on appeal, the claim must be set out in the appellant's notice and notice must be given to the Crown.[39]

---

31 CPR PD 16 para 16.1(2)(b), (c).
32 CPR PD 16 para 16.1(2)(d).
33 CPR 19.4A(3)(a).
34 See generally CPR Pt 17 for amending a statement of case.
35 CPR PD 16 para 16.2.
36 CPR PD 52 para 5.1A, which incorporates PD 16 para 16.1 (see above, paras 14.16–14.18).
37 CPR PD 52 para 7.3A.
38 CPR PD 52 paras 5.1A, 7.3A, which incorporate PD 16 para 16.2 (see above, para 14.22).
39 CPR PD 52 para 5.1B which incorporates 19.4A(3).

Notifying and joining the Crown

14.25   Provision is made for the Crown to be notified and – where it is not already a party to the proceedings – to be joined in two circumstances:

a)   where the court is considering making a declaration of incompatibility; and

b)   where the claim is for damages in respect of a judicial act.

Declarations of incompatibility

14.26   Where a court[40] is considering whether to make a declaration of incompatibility,[41] the Crown is entitled to notice[42] and no declaration may be made unless notice has been given.[43] The Crown is thus able to make representations and put forward arguments to the court before the declaration is made. There is, however, no requirement for the Crown to intervene; it has a choice whether or not to do so, which will no doubt depend upon the circumstances of the case including whether issues of general public importance are involved.

14.27   The court may consider whether notice should be given at any time,[44] but the question should usually be considered at the case management conference, when directions may be given as to the service and content of the notice.[45] In relation to an appeal, the issue should normally be addressed when permission to appeal is sought.[46]

14.28   There is no reason why the Crown should not apply to be joined in an appropriate case, even if – at that stage – the court has not been asked (or has not yet considered whether) to make a declaration of incompatibility, if it is probable that such a question will arise in the course of proceedings.[47] This is most likely to arise in the context of an appeal.

---

40   The 'court' in this context may be the trial court or an appeal court (provided it is capable of making a declaration: see declarations of incompatibility – jurisdiction, para 14.67 below: *Poplar HARCA Ltd v Donoghue* [2001] EWCA Civ 595; [2001] 3 WLR 183, CA, at para 20.

41   For the circumstances in which such declarations can be made, see paras 14.64–14.69, below.

42   HRA 1998 s5(1).

43   CPR 19.4A(1).

44   CPR PD 19A para 6.1.

45   CPR PD 19A para 6.2.

46   CPR PD 52 para 5.1B which applies CPR 19.4A and CPR PD 19A.

47   *R v A* [2001] 1 WLR 789, HL.

Notice to the Crown

14.29 Although the CPR provide for the Crown to be notified at the earliest opportunity, rather than just before a declaration of incompatibility is made, a party seeking a declaration is not required to give formal notice when the remedy is first sought. The decision to notify the Crown is one for the court alone and it may do so either where a party applies for a declaration or, where the court – of its own motion – decides that the proceedings raise an issue which may lead it to consider making one.[48]

14.30   Despite this, in order to give the Crown as much notice as possible, whenever a party seeking a declaration or acknowledges that a declaration may be made, he or she should give as much *informal* notice to the Crown, as is practical, of the proceedings and the issues involved.[49]

Who gives notice

14.31 Although the CPR make no provision for who is to give formal notice that the court is considering making a declaration of incompatibility,[50] it has been held that it should always be given by the court.[51]

Contents of the notice

14.32 The notice should normally include the directions given by the court and all the statements of case in the claim.[52] The form of the notice is not prescribed and is as directed by the court.[53] The parties can be required to assist in its preparation.[54] It is likely that, where the statements of case do not adequately identify the Convention right under consideration, the court will order this to be set out in the notice.

48 CPR PD 19A para 6.1. The court will be in the best position to provide the Crown with the requisite information to enable it to decide whether it wishes to be joined: see *Poplar HARCA Ltd v Donoghue*, see note 40 above, at para 20. It is also consistent with the philosophy underpinning the CPR that the court has prime responsibility for managing cases.

49 *Poplar HARCA Ltd v Donoghue*, see note 40 above, at para 20 of the judgment.

50 The relevant rule (CPR 19.4A) is silent on the issue and the practice direction puts it in the passive tense – '... the court may at any time consider whether notice should be given to the Crown ...': CPR PD 19 para 6.1.

51 *Poplar HARCA Ltd v Donoghue*, above, at para 20.

52 CPR PD 19A para 6.4(2); or similar documents in relation to appeals (eg, the appellant's notice): PD 52 para 5.1B.

53 CPR PD 19A para 6.4(2). Rather oddly, there is no express requirement that it must be in writing, but this may be implied by the use of the words 'the notice' and 'served'.

54 CPR PD 19A para 6.4(3).

Length of notice

14.33 Notice must be at least 21 days – or longer or shorter as the court directs.[55] In deciding its length, the court must strike a balance between allowing the Crown sufficient time to decide whether it wishes to be joined and not unduly delaying the case.

14.34 Although not provided for in the CPR, there would appear to be no reason why the Crown should not apply for an extension of time, if this is necessary.

Who is notice given to

14.35 If the court decides that the Crown should be notified, written notice must be given to the person named in a list[56] published by HM Treasury.[57] This sets out the government departments authorised to receive notice and the name and address of the solicitor for service. If it is not apparent which department is to be notified, notice should be given to the Attorney-General.[58]

14.36 Where the Crown is already a party to the proceedings in some other capacity, notice should nevertheless be given.[59]

14.37 A copy of the notice must also be served on all the parties to the proceedings.[60]

14.38 The court may give directions for service of the notice.[61]

Joinder of the Crown

14.39 Having received notice that the court is considering making a declaration of incompatibility, a minister (or a person nominated by him) has a right to be joined as a party to the proceedings. Entitlement to be joined is contingent on the Crown giving notice[62] to the court and to every other party, although the court can order otherwise.[63] This notice can be given at any time during the proceedings.[64] No provision

---

55 CPR 19.4A(1).
56 Made under Crown Proceedings Act 1947 (CPA 1947) s17 and dated 31 July 2000, it is appended to CPR Pt 19 but is only published in 'the White Book' (Civil Procedure) and not 'the Green Book' (Civil Court Practice).
57 CPR PD 19A para 6.4(1).
58 CPA 1947 s17(3).
59 *R v A* [2001] 1 WLR 789, HL; the purpose is to join the responsible minister.
60 CPR PD 19A para 6.4(2).
61 CPR PD 19A para 6.1.
62 HRA 1998 s5(2)(a).
63 CPR PD 19A para 6.5. This would enable the court to, say, dispense with notice in its entirety or with service on a party.
64 HRA 1998 5(3).

is made for it to be in a particular form or as to its contents.[65] Where the minister has nominated a person to be joined as a party, the notice must be accompanied by a written nomination.[66]

Claims for damages in respect of judicial acts[67]

14.40   A claim for damages in respect of a judicial act made in good faith must be made against the Crown[68] and not the individual judge concerned.[69] In addition, no award may be made unless the 'appropriate person' is joined.[70] The appropriate person is the minister responsible for the court concerned, or a person or government department nominated by him.[71] Accordingly, notice must also be given to the Crown where the claim is for damages in respect of a judicial act.[72]

14.41   The procedure is the same as where the court is considering making a declaration of incompatibility (see paras 14.26–14.39 above) with two modifications:[73]

a) the notice of the claim must be addressed to the Lord Chancellor and served on the Treasury Solicitor;[74] and

b) it must set out the details of the judicial act which is the subject of the claim for damages, and of the court or tribunal that made it.[75]

14.42   Where the appropriate person has not applied to be joined as a party within 21 days of being served with the notice (or such other period as the court directs), the court may join the appropriate person as a party (for instance, whether or not he or she wishes to be joined).[76]

---

65 CPR PD 19A para 6.5.

66 CPR PD 19A para 6.5.

67 See above, paras 13.47–13.49.

68 HRA 1998 9(4).

69 There is no restriction on suing the judge personally where the judicial act was not made in good faith.

70 HRA 1998 9(4); they do not have to be joined if already a party to the proceedings.

71 HRA 1998 s9(5).

72 CPR 19.4A(3)(b),

73 CPR PD 19A paras 6.1 to 6.6; see also CPR PD 28 para 1.2, CPR PD 29 para 1.2.

74 CPR PD 19A para 6.6(2); except where the judicial act is of a court-martial, in which case the appropriate person is the Secretary of State for Defence, but this is very unlikely to involve a housing case.

75 CPR PD 19A para 6.6(3).

76 CPR 19.4A(4).

The hearing

Which judges

The High Court

14.43   A deputy High Court judge, a Master or a district judge may not try a case in a claim made in respect of a judicial act or a claim for a declaration of incompatibility.[77]

County courts

14.44   A district judge or a Recorder may not try a case in a claim made in respect of a judicial act.[78] County courts have no jurisdiction to make declarations for incompatibility (see para 14.68, below).

Citation of Strasbourg authorities

14.45   If a party to proceedings needs to give evidence of any judgment, decision, declaration or opinion of the Strasbourg authorities which is to be taken into account by the court,[79] the authority must be an authoritative and complete report.[80] Copies of the complete original texts issued by the European Court and the Commission – either paper-based or from the Court's judgment database[81] – may be used.[82]

14.46   The party citing the authorities must provide the court and any other party to the proceedings with a list of them and copies of the reports not less than three days before the hearing.[83]

Evidence in claims in respect of judicial acts

14.47   Where the claim is for a remedy in respect of a judicial act which is alleged to be in violation of the claimant's article 5 Convention right (the right to liberty and security) and is based on a finding of a court

---

77   CPR PD 2B para 7A.
78   CPR PD 2B para 15.
79   Courts and tribunals must of course take into account the Strasbourg jurisprudence (see para 12.17, above): HRA 1998 s2(1).
80   CPR PD 39A para 8.1(1); whether it is 'authoritative and complete' is left to the discretion of the court.
81   HUDOC, which can be accessed on the internet at www.echr.coe.int.
82   CPR PD 39A para 8.1(3).
83   CPR PD 39A para 8.1(2).

or tribunal that the claimant's Convention right has been infringed, the finding of the other court or tribunal may be relied on as *prima facie* evidence that the authority acted unlawfully. It will nevertheless be open to the defendant to refute the finding on grounds of fact or law. The court hearing the claim, however, is not bound by the finding of the first court or tribunal. It may – if it wishes – proceed on the basis of that finding but is not required to do so; it may reach its own conclusion in the light of that finding and of the evidence heard by the first court or tribunal.[84]

14.48   On any application or appeal concerning, among other things, a committal order, if the court ordering the release of the person concludes that his or her Convention rights have been infringed by the making of the order to which the application or appeal relates, the judgment or order should say so. If it fails to do so, however, it does not prevent another court from deciding the matter.[85]

Adjournments to raise human rights issues

14.49   In general, the decision whether to adjourn a hearing in order to enable a party to present evidence in support of his or her case is a matter for the judge.[86]

14.50   Where, however, it is possible to give a decision summarily in a case where there will almost certainly be an appeal, it is not wrong to refuse an adjournment to allow a party to produce evidence in support of a human rights issue, as this approach avoids expense and delay being incurred at first instance and on appeal.[87]

Relief and remedies

14.51   Where a court finds that a public authority has acted[88] unlawfully by reason of incompatibility with a Convention right, it may grant such relief or remedy, or make such order, within its powers as it considers just and appropriate.[89] It follows that the HRA 1998 does not confer

---

84 CPR 33.9(2).
85 CPR PD 40B para 14.4.
86 CPR 3.1(2)(b).
87 *Poplar Housing and Regeneration Community Association Ltd v Donoghue* [2001] EWCA Civ 595; [2001] 3 WLR 183, CA, at paras 9–10.
88 Or proposes to act.
89 HRA 1998 s8(1).

on a court the power to grant relief or a remedy which it does not otherwise have, so, for instance, a magistrates' court cannot grant an injunction.

14.52   It is important to stress that there is no entitlement to a remedy for an infringement of a Convention right (even for damages[90]); that decision is always at the discretion of the particular court.[91]

Damages

Generally

14.53   Only a court which has the power to award damages or order the payment of compensation in civil proceedings may award damages against a public authority found to have acted incompatibly with a Convention right.[92]

14.54   There is no limit to the amount of any damages but no award may be made unless the court is satisfied that it is necessary to afford just satisfaction to the person in whose favour it is made. In making that decision, account must be taken of all the circumstances of the case, including:

a) any other relief or remedy granted, or order made in relation to the unlawful act in question (by that or any other court), and

b) the consequences of any decision (of that or any other court) in respect of the act.[93]

14.55   In deciding whether to make any award of damages and how much it should be, the court must take into account the principles applied by the ECtHR in relation to the award of compensation under article 41 of the Convention.[94] It should be noted that the obligation is, however, only to take account of ECtHR's principles and not to apply them strictly.

14.56   Article 41 provides for the injured party to be afforded 'just satisfaction' if there has been a violation of the Convention or its protocols and the state's internal law only allows partial reparation. The ECtHR awards just satisfaction under three heads of loss: pecuniary loss, non-pecuniary loss and costs and expenses.[95] It is not easy to extract

---

90 Contrary to the usual position in civil proceedings that a person who has suffered loss has a right to be compensated.

91 Indicated by the use of the word 'may' in HRA 1998 s8(1).

92 HRA 1998 s8(2), (6).

93 HRA 1998 s8(3).

94 HRA 1998 s8(4).

95 See paras 6.30–6.34, above. For a detailed discussion of these and examples of awards see *European Human Rights Law*, Starmer (LAG 1999), pp 61–72 and

clear principles on just satisfaction from the ECtHR's jurisprudence. The issue, however, has been the subject of a Law Commission report (*Damages under the Human Rights Act 1998*[96]) which cites with approval an analysis by Lord Woolf[97] of the ECtHR's approach. He suggests eight possible principles which may be summarised as follows:

1) If there is any other remedy in addition to damages, that other remedy should usually be granted initially and damages should only be granted in addition if necessary to afford just satisfaction.

2) The court should not award exemplary or aggravated damages.

3) An award should be 'of no greater sum than that necessary to achieve just satisfaction'. If it is necessary for a decision to be retaken, the court should wait and see what the outcome is.

4) The quantum of the award should be 'moderate' and 'normally on the low side by comparison to tortious awards'.

5) The award should be restricted to compensating the victim for what has happened 'so far as the unlawful conduct exceeds what could lawfully happen'.

6) The failure by the claimant to take preventative or remedial action will reduce the amount of damages.

7) There is no reason to distinguish between pecuniary and non-pecuniary loss. What matters is that the loss should be 'real [and] clearly caused by the conduct contrary to the Act'.

8) Domestic rules as to costs will probably cover any costs or expenses incurred by the complainant.

14.57   It is suggested that, given the authority of their source, these principles are likely to be very influential factors when courts make awards under the HRA 1998.

Damages in respect of judicial acts

14.58   Damages in respect of a judicial act, done in good faith, may not be awarded[98] otherwise than to compensate a person to the extent required by article 5(5) of the Convention,[99] which provides for victims of unlawful arrest or detention to have an enforceable right to compensation. It follows that a person wrongfully detained by a court

---

Human Rights Act 1998: A Practitioners Guide, Baker, ed, (Sweet & Maxwell, 1998) paras 2.25–2.27.

96 Law Com No 266.

97 *Judicial Review in International Perspective: II* (2000) Andenas and Fairgrieve (eds): *The Human Rights Act 1998 and Remedies* at p429.

98 Any award is against the Crown: HRA 1998 s9(4).

99 HRA 1998 s9(3).

order made in good faith has an enforceable right of compensation against the Crown.

14.59　Damages for judicial acts, which have been committed otherwise than in good faith, may be awarded without the article 5(5) limitation.

Injunctions

14.60　A court has the power to grant an injunction if it considers it just and equitable to do so. A successful litigant has no 'right' to an injunction. It is an equitable remedy and the court has an overriding discretion when deciding whether it is appropriate in a particular case. It follows that, as a general rule, final injunctions will only be granted where there is real danger that the behaviour which is the subject of the complaint will continue despite the court's ruling.

14.61　An injunction may be granted in respect of a claim under the HRA 1998. There is no reason why a court should not grant an injunction to prevent an anticipated breach of a Convention right or, as an interim measure, to preserve the status quo pending a trial, in which cases the normal rules apply.[101] The court, however, will be unlikely to grant injunctive relief where, for instance, it believes it is not necessary because the public authority will comply with a declaration, that they would find it impossible to comply with, it would be oppressive to do so, the breach is trivial, or some culpability attaches to the claimant.

Declaratory relief

14.62　Irrespective of the special power in HRA 1998 to make a declaration of incompatibility (see paras 14.64–14.67, below), courts have a general power to make declarations as to the correct legal position between the parties. As with injunctions, the grant of a declaration is discretionary.

14.63　It is suggested that it is important for HRA 1998 claimants to seek declaratory relief, because in actions against public authorities, courts may be reluctant to grant injunctions as authorities are expected to (and generally do) act lawfully when a court finds against them.

101　See CPR Pt 25 (interim remedies).

Declarations of incompatibility

14.64 The HRA 1998 s3(1) provides that, so far as it is possible to do so, primary and subordinate legislation must be read and given effect in a way that is compatible with the Convention rights[102] (see para 12.7, above). If it cannot be so read, the higher courts have the power to make a declaration of incompatibility. Declarations may be made in two different sets of circumstances:

a) where the court is satisfied that a particular provision of primary legislation is incompatible;[103] and

b) where a provision of subordinate legislation is incompatible with a Convention right, and the removal of that incompatibility is prevented by primary legislation.[104]

14.65 Where, despite applying HRA 1998 s3(1), a result cannot be achieved which is compatible with the Convention, the court is not obliged to grant a declaration of incompatibility. It has a discretion whether or not to do so and will be influenced by the usual considerations that apply to the grant of any declaration.[105]

14.66 If a declaration of incompatibility is made, it does not, however, affect the validity, continuing operation or enforcement of the provision in respect of which it is given, nor is it binding on the parties to the proceedings in which it is made.[106] It is, in effect, a signal to the government that the law needs amending.[107]

14.67 There appears to be no jurisdictional reason why an appellate court with the power to make a declaration for incompatibility cannot make one, even though the lower court was not asked to do so, quite possibly because that court was not able to grant it. So far as a declaration of incompatibility may arise on the application of a party to proceedings, the CPR certainly contemplate it[108] and, in *Wilson v First County Trust Ltd*,[109] the Court of Appeal did not doubt that it could

---

102 HRA 1998 s3(1).

103 HRA 1998 s4(2).

104 HRA 1998 s4(4).

105 *Poplar HARCA Ltd v Donoghue* [2001] EWCA Civ 595; [2001] 3 WLR 183, CA, at para 75.

106 HRA 1998 s4(6).

107 For instance, to consider taking remedial action under HRA 1998 s10.

108 See CPR PD 52 para 5.1A, which requires the party to include information about the human rights remedy (assuming a declaration of incompatibility is a 'remedy') sought in the appellant's notice.

109 [2001] 2 WLR 302, CA.

make such a declaration of its own motion (although the point does not seem to have been argued).[110] Nevertheless, it is suggested that the appellate court has a discretion whether or not to allow a party to seek such a declaration on appeal where it was not sought at first instance; relevant considerations would include the need for evidence, the general public importance of the alleged incompatibility and the interests of the Crown (who would have to be joined if the point were to be addressed).

Jurisdiction

14.68   Only certain courts[111] have the power to make declarations of incompatibility, in particular, the High Court, the Court of Appeal[112] and the House of Lords.[113] Provision is made, however, for a lower court to transfer proceedings to the High Court so that a declaration can be made.

Transfer to the High Court

14.69   The CPR make general provision for any claim to be transferred from a county court to the High Court.[114] The circumstances in which a transfer may be ordered include where the question of making a declaration of incompatibility arises.[115] This should only be done, however, where there is a real prospect of a declaration being made.[116]

Tribunal proceedings

14.70   For these purposes, a tribunal is any tribunal in which legal proceedings may be brought.[117]

---

110 And, indeed, it went on to make it: see *Wilson v First County Trust Ltd (No 2)* [2001] EWCA Civ 633; [2001] 3 WLR 42, CA.

111 Note also that deputy High Court judges, Masters or district judges may not try claims for declarations of incompatibility (see para 14.43, above).

112 Including the Courts-Martial Appeal Court.

113 HRA 1998 s4(5). The Judicial Committee of the Privy Council may also make declarations but it is unlikely to be relevant to housing cases.

114 See CPR Pt 30 (Transfer).

115 CPR 30.3(2)(g).

116 CPR PD 30 (para 7).

117 HRA 1998 s21(1) (see para 13.38, above).

Jurisdiction

14.71 There is no right to bring a human rights claim in a tribunal,[118] but reliance may be placed on human rights in tribunal proceedings.[119]

Procedure

14.72 To date, no rules have been promulgated for the purpose of varying the procedure of any tribunal concerned with housing issues in relation to the HRA 1998. Any person wishing to rely on human rights must therefore follow the normal procedure for the particular tribunal.

Relief and remedies

Generally

14.73 If a tribunal finds that there has been a violation of a Convention right by a public authority, it may only grant such relief or remedy, or make such order, within its powers as it considers just and appropriate.[120] It follows that the HRA 1998 does not confer on a tribunal the power to grant relief or a remedy which it does not otherwise have. For instance, a rent assessment committee cannot grant an injunction.

14.74 As with a court, there is no entitlement to a remedy for an infringement of a Convention right; that decision is always at the discretion of the particular tribunal (see para 14.52 above).

14.75 The powers of tribunals to grant relief or remedies may be augmented by ministerial order to the extent it is considered necessary to ensure that the tribunal can provide an appropriate remedy.[121] To date, no such orders have been made.

Damages

14.76 Only a tribunal which may order the payment of compensation has the power to award damages in respect of the unlawful act of a public authority.[122]

---

118 For instance, under HRA 1998 s7(1); although there is a power to extend jurisdiction to tribunals: see s7(11).
119 For instance, under HRA 1998 s7(2).
120 HRA 1998 s8(1).
121 HRA 1998 s7(11)(a).
122 HRA 1998 s8(2), (6).

Declarations of incompatibility

14.77   A tribunal has no power to make a declaration of incompatibility.[123] There is, however, no reason why a court hearing an appeal from a tribunal should not make such a declaration, provided that court has jurisdiction to do so (see para 14.67, above).

123 HRA 1998 s4(2), (5).

APPENDIX

Human Rights Act 1998

INTRODUCTION

The Convention Rights

1(1) In this Act 'the Convention rights' means the rights and fundamental freedoms set out in –

(a) Articles 2 to 12 and 14 of the Convention,
(b) Articles 1 to 3 of the First Protocol, and
(c) Articles 1 and 2 of the Sixth Protocol,

as read with Articles 16 to 18 of the Convention.

(2) Those Articles are to have effect for the purposes of this Act subject to any designated derogation or reservation (as to which see sections 14 and 15).

(3) The Articles are set out in Schedule 1.

(4) The Secretary of State may by order make such amendments to this Act as he considers appropriate to reflect the effect, in relation to the United Kingdom, of a protocol.

(5) In subsection (4) 'protocol' means a protocol to the Convention –

(a) which the United Kingdom has ratified; or
(b) which the United Kingdom has signed with a view to ratification.

(6) No amendment may be made by an order under subsection (4) so as to come into force before the protocol concerned is in force in relation to the United Kingdom.

Interpretation of Convention rights

2(1) A court or tribunal determining a question which has arisen in connection with a Convention right must take into account any –

(a) judgment, decision, declaration or advisory opinion of the European Court of Human Rights,
(b) opinion of the Commission given in a report adopted under Article 31 of the Convention,
(c) decision of the Commission in connection with Article 26 or 27(2) of the Convention, or
(d) decision of the Committee of Ministers taken under Article 46 of the Convention,

whenever made or given, so far as, in the opinion of the court or tribunal, it is relevant to the proceedings in which that question has arisen.

(2) Evidence of any judgment, decision, declaration or opinion of which account may have to be taken under this section is to be given in proceedings before

any court or tribunal in such manner as may be provided by rules.

(3)   In this section 'rules' means rules of court or, in the case of proceedings before a tribunal, rules made for the purposes of this section –

(a) by the Lord Chancellor or the Secretary of State, in relation to any proceedings outside Scotland;

(b) by the Secretary of State, in relation to proceedings in Scotland; or

(c) by a Northern Ireland department, in relation to proceedings before a tribunal in Northern Ireland –

(i)   which deals with transferred matters; and

(ii) for which no rules made under paragraph (a) are in force.

LEGISLATION
Interpretation of legislation

3(1)   So far as it is possible to do so, primary legislation and subordinate legislation must be read and given effect in a way which is compatible with the Convention rights.

(2)   This section –

(a) applies to primary legislation and subordinate legislation whenever enacted;

(b) does not affect the validity, continuing operation or enforcement of any incompatible primary legislation; and

(c) does not affect the validity, continuing operation or enforcement of any incompatible subordinate legislation if (disregarding any possibility of revocation) primary legislation prevents removal of the incompatibility.

Declaration of incompatibility

4(1)   Subsection (2) applies in any proceedings in which a court determines whether a provision of primary legislation is compatible with a Convention right.

(2)   If the court is satisfied that the provision is incompatible with a Convention right, it may make a declaration of that incompatibility.

(3)   Subsection (4) applies in any proceedings in which a court determines whether a provision of subordinate legislation, made in the exercise of a power conferred by primary legislation, is compatible with a Convention right.

(4)   If the court is satisfied –

(a) that the provision is incompatible with a Convention right, and

(b) that (disregarding any possibility of revocation) the primary legislation concerned prevents removal of the incompatibility,

it may make a declaration of that incompatibility.

(5)   In this section 'court' means –

(a) the House of Lords;

(b) the Judicial Committee of the Privy Council;

(c) the Courts-Martial Appeal Court;

(d) in Scotland, the High Court of Justiciary sitting otherwise than as a trial court or the Court of Session;

(e) in England and Wales or Northern Ireland, the High Court or the Court of Appeal.

(6) A declaration under this section ('a declaration of incompatibility') –

    (a) does not affect the validity, continuing operation or enforcement of the provision in respect of which it is given; and

    (b) is not binding on the parties to the proceedings in which it is made.

Right of Crown to intervene

5(1) Where a court is considering whether to make a declaration of incompatibility, the Crown is entitled to notice in accordance with rules of court.

(2) In any case to which subsection (1) applies –

    (a) a Minister of the Crown (or a person nominated by him),

    (b) a member of the Scottish Executive,

    (c) a Northern Ireland Minister,

    (d) a Northern Ireland department,

is entitled, on giving notice in accordance with rules of court, to be joined as a party to the proceedings.

(3) Notice under subsection (2) may be given at any time during the proceedings.

(4) A person who has been made a party to criminal proceedings (other than in Scotland) as the result of a notice under subsection (2) may, with leave, appeal to the House of Lords against any declaration of incompatibility made in the proceedings.

(5) In subsection (4) –

'criminal proceedings' includes all proceedings before the Courts-Martial Appeal Court; and

'leave' means leave granted by the court making the declaration of incompatibility or by the House of Lords.

PUBLIC AUTHORITIES

Acts of public authorities

6(1) It is unlawful for a public authority to act in a way which is incompatible with a Convention right.

(2) Subsection (1) does not apply to an act if –

    (a) as the result of one or more provisions of primary legislation, the authority could not have acted differently; or

    (b) in the case of one or more provisions of, or made under, primary legislation which cannot be read or given effect in a way which is compatible with the Convention rights, the authority was acting so as to give effect to or enforce those provisions.

(3) In this section 'public authority' includes –

    (a) a court or tribunal, and

    (b) any person certain of whose functions are functions of a public nature,

but does not include either House of Parliament or a person exercising functions in connection with proceedings in Parliament.

(4) In subsection (3) 'Parliament' does not include the House of Lords in its judicial capacity.

(5) In relation to a particular act, a person is not a public authority by virtue only of subsection (3)(b) if the nature of the act is private.

(6) 'An act' includes a failure to act but does not include a failure to –

(a) introduce in, or lay before, Parliament a proposal for legislation; or

(b) make any primary legislation or remedial order.

Proceedings

7(1) A person who claims that a public authority has acted (or proposes to act) in a way which is made unlawful by section 6(1) may –

(a) bring proceedings against the authority under this Act in the appropriate court or tribunal, or

(b) rely on the Convention right or rights concerned in any legal proceedings,

but only if he is (or would be) a victim of the unlawful act.

(2) In subsection (1)(a) 'appropriate court or tribunal' means such court or tribunal as may be determined in accordance with rules; and proceedings against an authority include a counterclaim or similar proceeding.

(3) If the proceedings are brought on an application for judicial review, the applicant is to be taken to have a sufficient interest in relation to the unlawful act only if he is, or would be, a victim of that act.

(4) If the proceedings are made by way of a petition for judicial review in Scotland, the applicant shall be taken to have title and interest to sue in relation to the unlawful act only if he is, or would be, a victim of that act.

(5) Proceedings under subsection (1)(a) must be brought before the end of –

(a) the period of one year beginning with the date on which the act complained of took place; or

(b) such longer period as the court or tribunal considers equitable having regard to all the circumstances,

but that is subject to any rule imposing a stricter time limit in relation to the procedure in question.

(6) In subsection (1)(b) 'legal proceedings' includes –

(a) proceedings brought by or at the instigation of a public authority; and

(b) an appeal against the decision of a court or tribunal.

(7) For the purposes of this section, a person is a victim of an unlawful act only if he would be a victim for the purposes of Article 34 of the Convention if proceedings were brought in the European Court of Human Rights in respect of that act.

(8) Nothing in this Act creates a criminal offence.

(9) In this section 'rules' means –

(a) in relation to proceedings before a court or tribunal outside Scotland, rules made by the Lord Chancellor or the Secretary of State for the purposes of this section or rules of court,

(b) in relation to proceedings before a court or tribunal in Scotland, rules made by the Secretary of State for those purposes,

(c) in relation to proceedings before a tribunal in Northern Ireland –

(i) which deals with transferred matters; and

(ii) for which no rules made under paragraph (a) are in force,

rules made by a Northern Ireland department for those purposes,

and includes provision made by order under section 1 of the Courts and Legal Services Act 1990.

(10) In making rules, regard must be had to section 9.

(11) The Minister who has power to make rules in relation to a particular tribunal may, to the extent he considers it necessary to ensure that the tribunal can provide an appropriate remedy in relation to an act (or proposed act) of a public authority which is (or would be) unlawful as a result of section 6(1), by order add to –

(a) the relief or remedies which the tribunal may grant; or

(b) the grounds on which it may grant any of them.

(12) An order made under subsection (11) may contain such incidental, supplemental, consequential or transitional provision as the Minister making it considers appropriate.

(13) 'The Minister' includes the Northern Ireland department concerned.

Judicial remedies

8(1) In relation to any act (or proposed act) of a public authority which the court finds is (or would be) unlawful, it may grant such relief or remedy, or make such order, within its powers as it considers just and appropriate.

(2) But damages may be awarded only by a court which has power to award damages, or to order the payment of compensation, in civil proceedings.

(3) No award of damages is to be made unless, taking account of all the circumstances of the case, including –

(a) any other relief or remedy granted, or order made, in relation to the act in question (by that or any other court), and

(b) the consequences of any decision (of that or any other court) in respect of that act,

the court is satisfied that the award is necessary to afford just satisfaction to the person in whose favour it is made.

(4) In determining –

(a) whether to award damages, or

(b) the amount of an award,

the court must take into account the principles applied by the European Court of Human Rights in relation to the award of compensation under Article 41 of the Convention.

(5) A public authority against which damages are awarded is to be treated –

(a) in Scotland, for the purposes of section 3 of the Law Reform (Miscellaneous Provisions) (Scotland) Act 1940 as if the award were made in an action of damages in which the authority has been found liable in respect of loss or damage to the person to whom the award is made;

(b) for the purposes of the Civil Liability (Contribution) Act 1978 as liable in respect of damage suffered by the person to whom the award is made.

(6) In this section –

'court' includes a tribunal;
'damages' means damages for an unlawful act of a public authority; and
'unlawful' means unlawful under section 6(1).

Judicial acts

9(1) Proceedings under section 7(1)(a) in respect of a judicial act may be brought
only –
(a) by exercising a right of appeal;
(b) on an application (in Scotland a petition) for judicial review; or
(c) in such other forum as may be prescribed by rules.

(2) That does not affect any rule of law which prevents a court from being the subject of judicial review.

(3) In proceedings under this Act in respect of a judicial act done in good faith,
damages may not be awarded otherwise than to compensate a person to the
extent required by Article 5(5) of the Convention.

(4) An award of damages permitted by subsection (3) is to be made against the
Crown; but no award may be made unless the appropriate person, if not a
party to the proceedings, is joined.

(5) In this section –
'appropriate person' means the Minister responsible for the court concerned,
or a person or government department nominated by him;
'court' includes a tribunal;
'judge' includes a member of a tribunal, a justice of the peace and a clerk or
other officer entitled to exercise the jurisdiction of a court;
'judicial act' means a judicial act of a court and includes an act done on the
instructions, or on behalf, of a judge; and
'rules' has the same meaning as in section 7(9).

REMEDIAL ACTION

Power to take remedial action

10(1) This section applies if –
(a) a provision of legislation has been declared under section 4 to be incompatible with a Convention right and, if an appeal lies –
(i) all persons who may appeal have stated in writing that they do not
intend to do so;
(ii) the time for bringing an appeal has expired and no appeal has been
brought within that time; or
(iii) an appeal brought within that time has been determined or abandoned; or
(b) it appears to a Minister of the Crown or Her Majesty in Council that,
having regard to a finding of the European Court of Human Rights made
after the coming into force of this section in proceedings against the
United Kingdom, a provision of legislation is incompatible with an
obligation of the United Kingdom arising from the Convention.

(2) If a Minister of the Crown considers that there are compelling reasons for proceeding under this section, he may by order make such amendments to the
legislation as he considers necessary to remove the incompatibility.

(3) If, in the case of subordinate legislation, a Minister of the Crown considers –

    (a) that it is necessary to amend the primary legislation under which the subordinate legislation in question was made, in order to enable the incompatibility to be removed, and

    (b) that there are compelling reasons for proceeding under this section,

he may by order make such amendments to the primary legislation as he considers necessary.

(4) This section also applies where the provision in question is in subordinate legislation and has been quashed, or declared invalid, by reason of incompatibility with a Convention right and the Minister proposes to proceed under paragraph 2(b) of Schedule 2.

(5) If the legislation is an Order in Council, the power conferred by subsection (2) or (3) is exercisable by Her Majesty in Council.

(6) In this section 'legislation' does not include a Measure of the Church Assembly or of the General Synod of the Church of England.

(7) Schedule 2 makes further provision about remedial orders.

OTHER RIGHTS AND PROCEEDINGS

Safeguard for existing human rights

11   A person's reliance on a Convention right does not restrict –

    (a) any other right or freedom conferred on him by or under any law having effect in any part of the United Kingdom; or

    (b) his right to make any claim or bring any proceedings which he could make or bring apart from sections 7 to 9.

Freedom of expression

12 (1) This section applies if a court is considering whether to grant any relief which, if granted, might affect the exercise of the Convention right to freedom of expression.

(2) If the person against whom the application for relief is made ('the respondent') is neither present nor represented, no such relief is to be granted unless the court is satisfied –

    (a) that the applicant has taken all practicable steps to notify the respondent; or

    (b) that there are compelling reasons why the respondent should not be notified.

(3) No such relief is to be granted so as to restrain publication before trial unless the court is satisfied that the applicant is likely to establish that publication should not be allowed.

(4) The court must have particular regard to the importance of the Convention right to freedom of expression and, where the proceedings relate to material which the respondent claims, or which appears to the court, to be journalistic, literary or artistic material (or to conduct connected with such material), to –

    (a) the extent to which –

       (i) the material has, or is about to, become available to the public; or

       (ii) it is, or would be, in the public interest for the material to be published;

(b) any relevant privacy code.

(5) In this section –

'court' includes a tribunal; and

'relief' includes any remedy or order (other than in criminal proceedings).

Freedom of thought, conscience and religion

13 (1) If a court's determination of any question arising under this Act might affect the exercise by a religious organisation (itself or its members collectively) of the Convention right to freedom of thought, conscience and religion, it must have particular regard to the importance of that right.

(2) In this section 'court' includes a tribunal.

DEROGATIONS AND RESERVATIONS

Derogations

14 (1) In this Act 'designated derogation' means any derogation by the United Kingdom from an Article of the Convention, or of any protocol to the Convention, which is designated for the purposes of this Act in an order made by the Secretary of State.

[(2) *repealed.*]

(3) If a designated derogation is amended or replaced it ceases to be a designated derogation.

(4) But subsection (3) does not prevent the Secretary of State from exercising his power under subsection (1) to make a fresh designation order in respect of the Article concerned.

(5) The Secretary of State must by order make such amendments to Schedule 3 as he considers appropriate to reflect –

(a) any designation order; or
(b) the effect of subsection (3).

(6) A designation order may be made in anticipation of the making by the United Kingdom of a proposed derogation.

Reservations

15 (1) In this Act 'designated reservation' means –

(a) the United Kingdom's reservation to Article 2 of the First Protocol to the Convention; and
(b) any other reservation by the United Kingdom to an Article of the Convention, or of any protocol to the Convention, which is designated for the purposes of this Act in an order made by the Secretary of State.

(2) The text of the reservation referred to in subsection (1)(a) is set out in Part II of Schedule 3.

(3) If a designated reservation is withdrawn wholly or in part it ceases to be a designated reservation.

(4) But subsection (3) does not prevent the Secretary of State from exercising his power under subsection (1)(b) to make a fresh designation order in respect of the Article concerned.

(5) The Secretary of State must by order make such amendments to this Act as he considers appropriate to reflect –

(a) any designation order; or
(b) the effect of subsection (3).

Period for which designated derogations have effect

16 (1) If it has not already been withdrawn by the United Kingdom, a designated derogation ceases to have effect for the purposes of this Act in the case of any other derogation, at the end of the period of five years beginning with the date on which the order designating it was made.

(2) At any time before the period –

(a) fixed by subsection (1), or
(b) extended by an order under this subsection,

comes to an end, the Secretary of State may by order extend it by a further period of five years.

(3) An order under section 14(1) ceases to have effect at the end of the period for consideration, unless a resolution has been passed by each House approving the order.

(4) Subsection (3) does not affect –

(a) anything done in reliance on the order; or
(b) the power to make a fresh order under section 14(1).

(5) In subsection (3) 'period for consideration' means the period of forty days beginning with the day on which the order was made.

(6) In calculating the period for consideration, no account is to be taken of any time during which –

(a) Parliament is dissolved or prorogued; or
(b) both Houses are adjourned for more than four days.

(7) If a designated derogation is withdrawn by the United Kingdom, the Secretary of State must by order make such amendments to this Act as he considers are required to reflect that withdrawal.

Periodic review of designated reservations

17 (1) The appropriate Minister must review the designated reservation referred to in section 15(1)(a) –

(a) before the end of the period of five years beginning with the date on which section 1(2) came into force; and
(b) if that designation is still in force, before the end of the period of five years beginning with the date on which the last report relating to it was laid under subsection (3).

(2) The appropriate Minister must review each of the other designated reservations (if any) –

(a) before the end of the period of five years beginning with the date on which the order designating the reservation first came into force; and
(b) if the designation is still in force, before the end of the period of five years beginning with the date on which the last report relating to it was laid under subsection (3).

(3)   The Minister conducting a review under this section must prepare a report on the result of the review and lay a copy of it before each House of Parliament.

Appointment to European Court of Human Rights

18 (1)   In this section 'judicial office' means the office of –

(a) Lord Justice of Appeal, Justice of the High Court or Circuit judge, in England and Wales;
(b) judge of the Court of Session or sheriff, in Scotland;
(c) Lord Justice of Appeal, judge of the High Court or county court judge, in Northern Ireland.

(2)   The holder of a judicial office may become a judge of the European Court of Human Rights ('the Court') without being required to relinquish his office.

(3)   But he is not required to perform the duties of his judicial office while he is a judge of the Court.

(4)   In respect of any period during which he is a judge of the Court –

(a) a Lord Justice of Appeal or Justice of the High Court is not to count as a judge of the relevant court for the purposes of section 2(1) or 4(1) of the Supreme Court Act 1981 (maximum number of judges) nor as a judge of the Supreme Court for the purposes of section 12(1) to (6) of that Act (salaries, etc);
(b) a judge of the Court of Session is not to count as a judge of that court for the purposes of section 1(1) of the Court of Session Act 1988 (maximum number of judges) or of section 9(1)(c) of the Administration of Justice Act 1973 ('the 1973 Act') (salaries, etc);
(c) a Lord Justice of Appeal or judge of the High Court in Northern Ireland is not to count as a judge of the relevant court for the purposes of section 2(1) or 3(1) of the Judicature (Northern Ireland) Act 1978 (maximum number of judges) nor as a judge of the Supreme Court of Northern Ireland for the purposes of section 9(1)(d) of the 1973 Act (salaries, etc);
(d) a Circuit judge is not to count as such for the purposes of section 18 of the Courts Act 1971 (salaries, etc);
(e) a sheriff is not to count as such for the purposes of section 14 of the Sheriff Courts (Scotland) Act 1907 (salaries, etc);
(f) a county court judge of Northern Ireland is not to count as such for the purposes of section 106 of the County Courts Act Northern Ireland) 1959 (salaries, etc).

(5)   If a sheriff principal is appointed a judge of the Court, section 11(1) of the Sheriff Courts (Scotland) Act 1971 (temporary appointment of sheriff principal) applies, while he holds that appointment, as if his office is vacant.

(6)   Schedule 4 makes provision about judicial pensions in relation to the holder of a judicial office who serves as a judge of the Court.

(7)   The Lord Chancellor or the Secretary of State may by order make such transitional provision (including, in particular, provision for a temporary increase in the maximum number of judges) as he considers appropriate in relation to any holder of a judicial office who has completed his service as a judge of the Court.

PARLIAMENTARY PROCEDURE
Statements of compatibility

19 (1)   A Minister of the Crown in charge of a Bill in either House of Parliament must, before Second Reading of the Bill –

    (a)   make a statement to the effect that in his view the provisions of the Bill are compatible with the Convention rights ('a statement of compatibility'); or

    (b)   make a statement to the effect that although he is unable to make a statement of compatibility the government nevertheless wishes the House to proceed with the Bill.

    (2)   The statement must be in writing and be published in such manner as the Minister making it considers appropriate.

SUPPLEMENTAL
Orders etc under this Act

20 (1)   Any power of a Minister of the Crown to make an order under this Act is exercisable by statutory instrument.

    (2)   The power of the Lord Chancellor or the Secretary of State to make rules (other than rules of court) under section 2(3) or 7(9) is exercisable by statutory instrument.

    (3)   Any statutory instrument made under section 14, 15 or 16(7) must be laid before Parliament.

    (4)   No order may be made by the Lord Chancellor or the Secretary of State under section 1(4), 7(11) or 16(2) unless a draft of the order has been laid before, and approved by, each House of Parliament.

    (5)   Any statutory instrument made under section 18(7) or Schedule 4, or to which subsection (2) applies, shall be subject to annulment in pursuance of a resolution of either House of Parliament.

    (6)   The power of a Northern Ireland department to make –

    (a)   rules under section 2(3)(c) or 7(9)(c), or

    (b)   an order under section 7(11),

is exercisable by statutory rule for the purposes of the Statutory Rules (Northern Ireland) Order 1979.

    (7)   Any rules made under section 2(3)(c) or 7(9)(c) shall be subject to negative resolution; and section 41(6) of the Interpretation Act Northern Ireland) 1954 (meaning of 'subject to negative resolution') shall apply as if the power to make the rules were conferred by an Act of the Northern Ireland Assembly.

    (8)   No order may be made by a Northern Ireland department under section 7(11) unless a draft of the order has been laid before, and approved by, the Northern Ireland Assembly.

Interpretation, etc

21 (1)   In this Act –

'amend' includes repeal and apply (with or without modifications);

'the appropriate Minister' means the Minister of the Crown having charge of the appropriate authorised government department (within the meaning of the Crown Proceedings Act 1947);

'the Commission' means the European Commission of Human Rights;

'the Convention' means the Convention for the Protection of Human Rights and Fundamental Freedoms, agreed by the Council of Europe at Rome on 4th November 1950 as it has effect for the time being in relation to the United Kingdom;

'declaration of incompatibility' means a declaration under section 4;

'Minister of the Crown' has the same meaning as in the Ministers of the Crown Act 1975;

'Northern Ireland Minister' includes the First Minister and the deputy First Minister in Northern Ireland;

'primary legislation' means any –

(a) public general Act;

(b) local and personal Act;

(c) private Act;

(d) Measure of the Church Assembly;

(e) Measure of the General Synod of the Church of England;

(f) Order in Council –

   (i) made in exercise of Her Majesty's Royal Prerogative;

   (ii) made under section 38(1)(a) of the Northern Ireland Constitution Act 1973 or the corresponding provision of the Northern Ireland Act 1998; or

   (iii) amending an Act of a kind mentioned in paragraph (a), (b) or (c);

and includes an order or other instrument made under primary legislation (otherwise than by the National Assembly for Wales, a member of the Scottish Executive, a Northern Ireland Minister or a Northern Ireland department) to the extent to which it operates to bring one or more provisions of that legislation into force or amends any primary legislation;

'the First Protocol' means the protocol to the Convention agreed at Paris on 20th March 1952;

'the Sixth Protocol' means the protocol to the Convention agreed at Strasbourg on 28th April 1983;

'the Eleventh Protocol' means the protocol to the Convention (restructuring the control machinery established by the Convention) agreed at Strasbourg on 11th May 1994;

'remedial order' means an order under section 10;

'subordinate legislation' means any –

(a) Order in Council other than one –

   (i) made in exercise of Her Majesty's Royal Prerogative;

   (ii) made under section 38(1)(a) of the Northern Ireland Constitution Act 1973 or the corresponding provision of the Northern Ireland Act 1998; or

   (iii) amending an Act of a kind mentioned in the definition of primary legislation;

(b) Act of the Scottish Parliament;

(c) Act of the Parliament of Northern Ireland;

(d) Measure of the Assembly established under section 1 of the Northern Ireland Assembly Act 1973;

(e) Act of the Northern Ireland Assembly;
(f) order, rules, regulations, scheme, warrant, byelaw or other instrument made under primary legislation (except to the extent to which it operates to bring one or more provisions of that legislation into force or amends any primary legislation);
(g) order, rules, regulations, scheme, warrant, byelaw or other instrument made under legislation mentioned in paragraph (b), (c), (d) or (e) or made under an Order in Council applying only to Northern Ireland;
(h) order, rules, regulations, scheme, warrant, byelaw or other instrument made by a member of the Scottish Executive, a Northern Ireland Minister or a Northern Ireland department in exercise of prerogative or other executive functions of Her Majesty which are exercisable by such a person on behalf of Her Majesty;

'transferred matters' has the same meaning as in the Northern Ireland Act 1998; and

'tribunal' means any tribunal in which legal proceedings may be brought.

(2) The references in paragraphs (b) and (c) of section 2(1) to Articles are to Articles of the Convention as they had effect immediately before the coming into force of the Eleventh Protocol.

(3) The reference in paragraph (d) of section 2(1) to Article 46 includes a reference to Articles 32 and 54 of the Convention as they had effect immediately before the coming into force of the Eleventh Protocol.

(4) The references in section 2(1) to a report or decision of the Commission or a decision of the Committee of Ministers include references to a report or decision made as provided by paragraphs 3, 4 and 6 of Article 5 of the Eleventh Protocol (transitional provisions).

(5) Any liability under the Army Act 1955, the Air Force Act 1955 or the Naval Discipline Act 1957 to suffer death for an offence is replaced by a liability to imprisonment for life or any less punishment authorised by those Acts; and those Acts shall accordingly have effect with the necessary modifications.

Short title, commencement, application and extent

22 (1) This Act may be cited as the Human Rights Act 1998.

(2) Sections 18, 20 and 21(5) and this section come into force on the passing of this Act.

(3) The other provisions of this Act come into force on such day as the Secretary of State may by order appoint; and different days may be appointed for different purposes.

(4) Paragraph (b) of subsection (1) of section 7 applies to proceedings brought by or at the instigation of a public authority whenever the act in question took place; but otherwise that subsection does not apply to an act taking place before the coming into force of that section.

(5) This Act binds the Crown.

(6) This Act extends to Northern Ireland.

(7) Section 21(5), so far as it relates to any provision contained in the Army Act 1955, the Air Force Act 1955 or the Naval Discipline Act 1957, extends to any place to which that provision extends.

SCHEDULE 1: THE ARTICLES

PART I: THE CONVENTION: RIGHTS AND FREEDOMS
Article 2: Right to life
1 Everyone's right to life shall be protected by law. No one shall be deprived of his life intentionally save in the execution of a sentence of a court following his conviction of a crime for which this penalty is provided by law.
2 Deprivation of life shall not be regarded as inflicted in contravention of this Article when it results from the use of force which is no more than absolutely necessary:
   (a) in defence of any person from unlawful violence;
   (b) in order to effect a lawful arrest or to prevent the escape of a person lawfully detained;
   (c) in action lawfully taken for the purpose of quelling a riot or insurrection.

Article 3: Prohibition of torture
No one shall be subjected to torture or to inhuman or degrading treatment or punishment.

Article 4: Prohibition of slavery and forced labour
1 No one shall be held in slavery or servitude.
2 No one shall be required to perform forced or compulsory labour.
3 For the purpose of this Article the term 'forced or compulsory labour' shall not include:
   (a) any work required to be done in the ordinary course of detention imposed according to the provisions of Article 5 of this Convention or during conditional release from such detention;
   (b) any service of a military character or, in case of conscientious objectors in countries where they are recognised, service exacted instead of compulsory military service;
   (c) any service exacted in case of an emergency or calamity threatening the life or well-being of the community;
   (d) any work or service which forms part of normal civic obligations.

Article 5: Right to liberty and security
1 Everyone has the right to liberty and security of person. No one shall be deprived of his liberty save in the following cases and in accordance with a procedure prescribed by law:
   (a) the lawful detention of a person after conviction by a competent court;
   (b) the lawful arrest or detention of a person for non-compliance with the lawful order of a court or in order to secure the fulfilment of any obligation prescribed by law;
   (c) the lawful arrest or detention of a person effected for the purpose of bringing him before the competent legal authority on reasonable suspicion of having committed an offence or when it is reasonably considered necessary to prevent his committing an offence or fleeing after having done so;
   (d) the detention of a minor by lawful order for the purpose of educational

supervision or his lawful detention for the purpose of bringing him before the competent legal authority;

(e) the lawful detention of persons for the prevention of the spreading of infectious diseases, of persons of unsound mind, alcoholics or drug addicts or vagrants;

(f) the lawful arrest or detention of a person to prevent his effecting an unauthorised entry into the country or of a person against whom action is being taken with a view to deportation or extradition.

2 Everyone who is arrested shall be informed promptly, in a language which he understands, of the reasons for his arrest and of any charge against him.

3 Everyone arrested or detained in accordance with the provisions of paragraph 1(c) of this Article shall be brought promptly before a judge or other officer authorised by law to exercise judicial power and shall be entitled to trial within a reasonable time or to release pending trial. Release may be conditioned by guarantees to appear for trial.

4 Everyone who is deprived of his liberty by arrest or detention shall be entitled to take proceedings by which the lawfulness of his detention shall be decided speedily by a court and his release ordered if the detention is not lawful.

5 Everyone who has been the victim of arrest or detention in contravention of the provisions of this Article shall have an enforceable right to compensation.

Article 6: Right to a fair trial

1 In the determination of his civil rights and obligations or of any criminal charge against him, everyone is entitled to a fair and public hearing within a reasonable time by an independent and impartial tribunal established by law. Judgment shall be pronounced publicly but the press and public may be excluded from all or part of the trial in the interest of morals, public order or national security in a democratic society, where the interests of juveniles or the protection of the private life of the parties so require, or to the extent strictly necessary in the opinion of the court in special circumstances where publicity would prejudice the interests of justice.

2 Everyone charged with a criminal offence shall be presumed innocent until proved guilty according to law.

3 Everyone charged with a criminal offence has the following minimum rights:

(a) to be informed promptly, in a language which he understands and in detail, of the nature and cause of the accusation against him;

(b) to have adequate time and facilities for the preparation of his defence;

(c) to defend himself in person or through legal assistance of his own choosing or, if he has not sufficient means to pay for legal assistance, to be given it free when the interests of justice so require;

(d) to examine or have examined witnesses against him and to obtain the attendance and examination of witnesses on his behalf under the same conditions as witnesses against him;

(e) to have the free assistance of an interpreter if he cannot understand or speak the language used in court.

Article 7: No punishment without law

1 No one shall be held guilty of any criminal offence on account of any act or omission which did not constitute a criminal offence under national or international law at the time when it was committed. Nor shall a heavier penalty be imposed than the one that was applicable at the time the criminal offence was committed.

2 This Article shall not prejudice the trial and punishment of any person for any act or omission which, at the time when it was committed, was criminal according to the general principles of law recognised by civilised nations.

Article 8: Right to respect for private and family life

1 Everyone has the right to respect for his private and family life, his home and his correspondence.

2 There shall be no interference by a public authority with the exercise of this right except such as is in accordance with the law and is necessary in a democratic society in the interests of national security, public safety or the economic well-being of the country, for the prevention of disorder or crime, for the protection of health or morals, or for the protection of the rights and freedoms of others.

Article 9: Freedom of thought, conscience and religion

1 Everyone has the right to freedom of thought, conscience and religion; this right includes freedom to change his religion or belief and freedom, either alone or in community with others and in public or private, to manifest his religion or belief, in worship, teaching, practice and observance.

2 Freedom to manifest one's religion or beliefs shall be subject only to such limitations as are prescribed by law and are necessary in a democratic society in the interests of public safety, for the protection of public order, health or morals, or for the protection of the rights and freedoms of others.

Article 10: Freedom of expression

1 Everyone has the right to freedom of expression. This right shall include freedom to hold opinions and to receive and impart information and ideas without interference by public authority and regardless of frontiers. This Article shall not prevent States from requiring the licensing of broadcasting, television or cinema enterprises.

2 The exercise of these freedoms, since it carries with it duties and responsibilities, may be subject to such formalities, conditions, restrictions or penalties as are prescribed by law and are necessary in a democratic society, in the interests of national security, territorial integrity or public safety, for the prevention of disorder or crime, for the protection of health or morals, for the protection of the reputation or rights of others, for preventing the disclosure of information received in confidence, or for maintaining the authority and impartiality of the judiciary.

Article 11: Freedom of assembly and association

1 Everyone has the right to freedom of peaceful assembly and to freedom of

association with others, including the right to form and to join trade unions for the protection of his interests.

2 No restrictions shall be placed on the exercise of these rights other than such as are prescribed by law and are necessary in a democratic society in the interests of national security or public safety, for the prevention of disorder or crime, for the protection of health or morals or for the protection of the rights and freedoms of others. This Article shall not prevent the imposition of lawful restrictions on the exercise of these rights by members of the armed forces, of the police or of the administration of the State.

Article 12: Right to marry

Men and women of marriageable age have the right to marry and to found a family, according to the national laws governing the exercise of this right.

Article 14: Prohibition of discrimination

The enjoyment of the rights and freedoms set forth in this Convention shall be secured without discrimination on any ground such as sex, race, colour, language, religion, political or other opinion, national or social origin, association with a national minority, property, birth or other status.

Article 16: Restrictions on political activity of aliens

Nothing in Articles 10, 11 and 14 shall be regarded as preventing the High Contracting Parties from imposing restrictions on the political activity of aliens.

Article 17: Prohibition of abuse of rights

Nothing in this Convention may be interpreted as implying for any State, group or person any right to engage in any activity or perform any act aimed at the destruction of any of the rights and freedoms set forth herein or at their limitation to a greater extent than is provided for in the Convention.

Article 18: Limitation on use of restrictions on rights

The restrictions permitted under this Convention to the said rights and freedoms shall not be applied for any purpose other than those for which they have been prescribed.

PART II: THE FIRST PROTOCOL

Article 1: Protection of property

Every natural or legal person is entitled to the peaceful enjoyment of his possessions. No one shall be deprived of his possessions except in the public interest and subject to the conditions provided for by law and by the general principles of international law.

The preceding provisions shall not, however, in any way impair the right of a State to enforce such laws as it deems necessary to control the use of property in accordance with the general interest or to secure the payment of taxes or other contributions or penalties.

Article 2: Right to education

No person shall be denied the right to education. In the exercise of any functions which it assumes in relation to education and to teaching, the State shall respect the right of parents to ensure such education and teaching in conformity with their own religious and philosophical convictions.

Article 3: Right to free elections

The High Contracting Parties undertake to hold free elections at reasonable intervals by secret ballot, under conditions which will ensure the free expression of the opinion of the people in the choice of the legislature.

PART III: THE SIXTH PROTOCOL

Article 1: Abolition of the death penalty

The death penalty shall be abolished. No one shall be condemned to such penalty or executed.

Article 2: Death penalty in time of war

A State may make provision in its law for the death penalty in respect of acts committed in time of war or of imminent threat of war; such penalty shall be applied only in the instances laid down in the law and in accordance with its provisions. The State shall communicate to the Secretary General of the Council of Europe the relevant provisions of that law.

SCHEDULE 2: REMEDIAL ORDERS

Orders

1(1) A remedial order may –

    (a) contain such incidental, supplemental, consequential or transitional provision as the person making it considers appropriate;

    (b) be made so as to have effect from a date earlier than that on which it is made;

    (c) make provision for the delegation of specific functions;

    (d) make different provision for different cases.

(2) The power conferred by sub-paragraph (1)(a) includes –

    (a) power to amend primary legislation (including primary legislation other than that which contains the incompatible provision); and

    (b) power to amend or revoke subordinate legislation (including subordinate legislation other than that which contains the incompatible provision).

(3) A remedial order may be made so as to have the same extent as the legislation which it affects.

(4) No person is to be guilty of an offence solely as a result of the retrospective effect of a remedial order.

Procedure

2 No remedial order may be made unless –

    (a) a draft of the order has been approved by a resolution of each House of

Parliament made after the end of the period of 60 days beginning with the day on which the draft was laid; or

(b) it is declared in the order that it appears to the person making it that, because of the urgency of the matter, it is necessary to make the order without a draft being so approved.

Orders laid in draft

3(1) No draft may be laid under paragraph 2(a) unless –

(a) the person proposing to make the order has laid before Parliament a document which contains a draft of the proposed order and the required information; and

(b) the period of 60 days, beginning with the day on which the document required by this sub-paragraph was laid, has ended.

(2) If representations have been made during that period, the draft laid under paragraph 2(a) must be accompanied by a statement containing –

(a) a summary of the representations; and

(b) if, as a result of the representations, the proposed order has been changed, details of the changes.

Urgent cases

4(1) If a remedial order ('the original order') is made without being approved in draft, the person making it must lay it before Parliament, accompanied by the required information, after it is made.

(2) If representations have been made during the period of 60 days beginning with the day on which the original order was made, the person making it must (after the end of that period) lay before Parliament a statement containing –

(a) a summary of the representations; and

(b) if, as a result of the representations, he considers it appropriate to make changes to the original order, details of the changes.

(3) If sub-paragraph (2)(b) applies, the person making the statement must –

(a) make a further remedial order replacing the original order; and

(b) lay the replacement order before Parliament.

(4) If, at the end of the period of 120 days beginning with the day on which the original order was made, a resolution has not been passed by each House approving the original or replacement order, the order ceases to have effect (but without that affecting anything previously done under either order or the power to make a fresh remedial order).

Definitions

5 In this Schedule –

'representations' means representations about a remedial order (or proposed remedial order) made to the person making (or proposing to make) it and includes any relevant Parliamentary report or resolution; and

'required information' means –

(a) an explanation of the incompatibility which the order (or proposed order) seeks to remove, including particulars of the relevant declaration, finding or order; and

(b) a statement of the reasons for proceeding under section 10 and for making an order in those terms.

Calculating periods

6 In calculating any period for the purposes of this Schedule, no account is to be
taken of any time during which –

(a) Parliament is dissolved or prorogued; or
(b) both Houses are adjourned for more than four days.

7(1) This paragraph applies in relation to –

(a) any remedial order made, and any draft of such an order proposed to be
made –
(i)   by the Scottish Ministers; or
(ii) within devolved competence (within the meaning of the Scotland Act
1998) by Her Majesty in Council; and
(b) any document or statement to be laid in connection with such an order (or
proposed order).

(2) This Schedule has effect in relation to any such order (or proposed order), document or statement subject to the following modifications.

(3) Any reference to Parliament, each House of Parliament or both Houses of
Parliament shall be construed as a reference to the Scottish Parliament.

(4) Paragraph 6 does not apply and instead, in calculating any period for the purposes of this Schedule, no account is to be taken of any time during which the
Scottish Parliament is dissolved or is in recess for more than four days.

SCHEDULE 3: RESERVATION

[PART I: DEROGATION repealed by SI 2001 No 1216]

PART II: RESERVATION

At the time of signing the present (First) Protocol, I declare that, in view of certain provisions of the Education Acts in the United Kingdom, the principle
affirmed in the second sentence of Article 2 is accepted by the United
Kingdom only so far as it is compatible with the provision of efficient instruc-
tion and training, and the avoidance of unreasonable public expenditure.

Dated 20 March 1952. Made by the United Kingdom Permanent Representative to the Council of Europe.

SCHEDULE 4: JUDICIAL PENSIONS

Duty to make orders about pensions

1(1) The appropriate Minister must by order make provision with respect to pensions payable to or in respect of any holder of a judicial office who serves as an
ECHR judge.

(2) A pensions order must include such provision as the Minister making it considers is necessary to secure that –

(a) an ECHR judge who was, immediately before his appointment as an

ECHR judge, a member of a judicial pension scheme is entitled to remain as a member of that scheme;

(b) the terms on which he remains a member of the scheme are those which would have been applicable had he not been appointed as an ECHR judge; and

(c) entitlement to benefits payable in accordance with the scheme continues to be determined as if, while serving as an ECHR judge, his salary was that which would (but for section 18(4)) have been payable to him in respect of his continuing service as the holder of his judicial office.

Contributions

2 A pensions order may, in particular, make provision –

(a) for any contributions which are payable by a person who remains a member of a scheme as a result of the order, and which would otherwise be payable by deduction from his salary, to be made otherwise than by deduction from his salary as an ECHR judge; and

(b) for such contributions to be collected in such manner as may be determined by the administrators of the scheme.

Amendments of other enactments

3 A pensions order may amend any provision of, or made under, a pensions Act in such manner and to such extent as the Minister making the order considers necessary or expedient to ensure the proper administration of any scheme to which it relates.

Definitions

4 In this Schedule –
'appropriate Minister' means –

(a) in relation to any judicial office whose jurisdiction is exercisable exclusively in relation to Scotland, the Secretary of State; and

(b) otherwise, the Lord Chancellor;

'ECHR judge' means the holder of a judicial office who is serving as a judge of the Court;

'judicial pension scheme' means a scheme established by and in accordance with a pensions Act;

'pensions Act' means –

(a) the County Courts Act (Northern Ireland) 1959;

(b) the Sheriffs' Pensions (Scotland) Act 1961;

(c) the Judicial Pensions Act 1981; or

(d) the Judicial Pensions and Retirement Act 1993; and

'pensions order' means an order made under paragraph 1.

Index

LAG

Legal Action Group

Working with lawyers and advisers to promote equal access to justice

Legal Action magazine
The only monthly magazine published specifically for legal aid practitioners and the advice sector. Features 'Recent developments in housing law' every month.

2001 annual subscription: £77
Concessionary rates available for students and trainees – call the LAG office for details.

Books
LAG's catalogue includes a range of titles covering:

- community care
- crime
- debt
- education
- employment
- family
- housing
- human rights
- immigration
- personal injury
- practice & procedure
- welfare benefits
- LAG policy

Community Care Law Reports
The only law reports devoted entirely to community care issues. Compiled by an expert team and published quarterly, each issue contains:

- editorial review
- community care law update
- law reports
- cumulative index
- full tables

Training
Accredited with the Law Society, the Bar Council and the Institute of Legal executives, LAG provides training courses for housing practitioners at all levels of experience.

Conferences
LAG runs major conferences to examine issues at the cutting-edge of legal services policy and to inform practitioners of their implications.

For further information about any of Legal Action Group's activities, please contact:

Legal Action Group
242 Pentonville Road
London N1 9UN

DX 130400 London (Pentonville Road)
Telephone: 020 7833 2931
Fax: 020 7837 6094
e-mail: lag@lag.org.uk
www.lag.org.uk